Anonymous

Crown Hill cemetery

Anonymous

Crown Hill cemetery

ISBN/EAN: 9783337268831

Printed in Europe, USA, Canada, Australia, Japan

Cover: Foto ©Andreas Hilbeck / pixelio.de

More available books at **www.hansebooks.com**

OFFICE BUILDING.

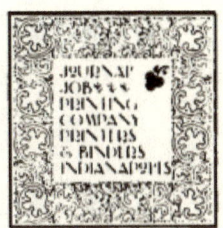

1397233

CONTENTS.
1896

	PAGE
ORIGINAL OFFICERS	7
OFFICERS, 1875	9
OFFICERS, 1888	11
OFFICERS, 1896	13
LIST OF CORPORATORS	15
INTRODUCTORY ARTICLE	17
ARTICLES OF ASSOCIATION	19
RULES AND REGULATIONS	25
LIST OF LOT-HOLDERS	33

ORIGINAL OFFICERS, 1863.

BOARD OF MANAGERS.

James M. Ray, W. S. Hubbard,
James Blake, W. H. Talbot,
S. A. Fletcher, Jr., John C. New,
Theodore P. Haughey.

PRESIDENT OF BOARD.
James M. Ray.

TREASURER.
S. A. Fletcher, Jr.

SECRETARY.
Theodore P. Haughey.

SUPERINTENDENT.
Frederick W. Chislett.

OFFICERS FOR 1875.

BOARD OF MANAGERS.

James M. Ray,
William S. Hubbard,
Thomas A. Morris,
John C. New,
S. A. Fletcher, Jr.,
Nicholas McCarty,
Theodore P. Haughey.

PRESIDENT OF BOARD.
Stoughton A. Fletcher, Jr.

TREASURER.
John C. New.

SECRETARY.
George P. Anderson.

SUPERINTENDENT.
Frederick W. Chislett.

OFFICERS FOR 1888.

BOARD OF MANAGERS.

THOMAS A. MORRIS, NICHOLAS MCCARTY,
S. A. FLETCHER, JR., JOHN C. NEW,
WILLIAM S. HUBBARD, WILLIAM WALLACE,
THEODORE P. HAUGHEY.

PRESIDENT OF BOARD
STOUGHTON A. FLETCHER, JR.

TREASURER.
JOHN C. NEW.

SECRETARY.
GEORGE P. ANDERSON.

SUPERINTENDENT.
FREDERICK W. CHISLETT.

OFFICERS FOR 1896.

BOARD OF MANAGERS.

Allen M. Fletcher,   Nicholas McCarty,
Thomas A. Morris,   John C. New,
William S. Hubbard,   John M. Kitchen,
George B. Vandes.

PRESIDENT OF BOARD.
Allen M. Fletcher.

TREASURER.   **SECRETARY.**
John C. New.   George P. Anderson.

SUPERINTENDENT.
Frederick W. Chislett.

LIST OF CORPORATORS.

Original Corporators.
1863.

JAMES M. RAY.
JAMES BLAKE.
CALVIN FLETCHER.
WILLIAM H. MORRISON.
THOMAS H. SHARPE.
W. O. ROCKWOOD.
WILLIAM S. HUBBARD.
ALMUS E. VINTON.
THEO. P. HAUGHEY.
S. A. FLETCHER, JR.
JOHN C. NEW.
NICHOLAS MCCARTY.
WILLIAM WALLACE.
JOHN M. LORD.
THOMAS A. MORRIS.
JOHN ARMSTRONG.
JESSE D. CARMICHAEL.
CHARLES N. TODD.
WILLIAM SHEETS.
JOHN M. KITCHEN.
ROBERT BROWNING.
ADDISON L. ROACHE.
GEORGE TOUSEY.
OVID BUTLER.
JOHN H. VAJEN.
E. B. MARTINDALE.
HERMAN LIEBER.
DANIEL YANDES.
JACOB A. CROSSLAND.
JOHN LOVE.

Present Corporators.
1896.

H. G. C. BALS.
ALLEN M. FLETCHER.
L. S. AYRES.
P. H. JAMESON.
BENJAMIN HARRISON.
JOHN S. SPANN.
WM. S. HUBBARD.
H. H. HANNA.
JOHN S. DUNCAN.
JOHN F. WALLICK.
JOHN C. NEW.
NICHOLAS MCCARTY.
JOHN R. ELDER.
JOHN H. HOLLIDAY.
THOMAS A. MORRIS.
JOHN ARMSTRONG.
WM. N. JACKSON.
GEORGE B. YANDES.
JOHN M. KITCHEN.
O. S. RUNNELS.
ADDISON L. ROACHE.
E. F. CLAYPOOL.
WM. J. HOLLIDAY.
JOHN H. VAJEN.
E. B. MARTINDALE.
HERMAN LIEBER.
JOHN COBURN.
FRED. RAND.
HERVEY BATES.

MAIN ENTRANCE—OUTSIDE VIEW.

INTRODUCTION.

IN presenting this publication, the managers of Crown Hill Cemetery hope to give to all those interested some idea of its growth and progress in later years, and more especially since 1888, when the last book was issued. A comparison of the two shows an increase in the number of lot-owners for the past eight (8) years of 2,208; the former book contained 3,793 and the present one 6,001 names.

Changes have been made in the rules and regulations which restrict individual display both in floral and monumental work, the excellent effect of which in promoting unity of design is well seen in the accompanying illustrations. The lawn plan, now enforced in most of the modern cemeteries, being especially adapted to the character of our landscape, was adopted in the very beginning as the fundamental scheme of all improvements, and the carrying out of this plan, subject only to the few changes that experience has proved to be necessary, places Crown Hill to-day in the front rank of modern rural cemeteries.

A brief sketch of the origin, organization and mode of management of this corporation forms a fit introduction to the present work. For some years before its foundation it was so obvious that the old grave-yard known as Greenlawn would soon be inadequate to the needs of the city that suggestions of new sites and larger areas for this purpose were frequently made, but formal action in the matter was not taken until the Fall of 1863. Three pioneer citizens, who had been chiefly concerned in the planning and extension of the old grave-yard, took lead in the far greater work of establishing the new one. Calvin Fletcher, Sr., James M. Ray and James Blake, having interested a few other citizens in the project, invited John Chislett of Pittsburg, Pa., to be present and address a meeting called by them on the 12th of September, 1863.

Gen. Thomas A. Morris, Wm. S. Hubbard, Theodore P. Haughey, A. L. Roache, John C. New, S. A. Fletcher, Jr., Herman Lieber, J. D. Carmichael, James Blake and James M. Ray, attended the meeting. Aided by the advice of Mr. Chislett, committees were appointed to select a site, perfect plans and prepare for incorporation, which was finally completed under the statute on the 25th of September, 1863, with thirty incorporators. The Crown Hill site was purchased; additional ground has been added since to the original purchase, so that it now comprises 464 acres, making one of the largest cemeteries in the United States. Mr. Frederick W. Chislett, son of Mr. John Chislett, was elected superintendent and work was begun as soon as possible. On the 1st of June, 1864, Crown Hill was dedicated with appropriate ceremonies, including an address by Hon. Albert S. White, Ex-United States Senator and Judge of the Federal District Court of the United States. The fundamental principle of the organization is that all money received from sale of lots must be applied to maintain and improve the grounds; this is unalterable, and a final assurance to all concerned that the Cemetery can never be perverted to selfish or speculative abuses.

The Board of Incorporators is self-perpetuating, the members filling all vacancies at their pleasure and electing the Board of Managers annually. Upon these principles the management has been undeviatingly conducted with a success far exceeding the expectations of the most sanguine.

Since the last report was issued important changes have been made; the main entrance and office has been moved to the east side of the Cemetery, and the handsome stone gateway, with adjoining commodious offices, has been erected. The adjacent grounds have had their great natural beauty developed and made accessible by walks and drives, and the policy of the management to have this part of the Cemetery used only for ornamentation and park purposes, fully carried out. A water plant has also been added, furnishing ample facilities for sprinkling the drives and keeping them in excellent condition, free from dust at all seasons of the year. Two lines of electric cars, one on each side of the grounds, have greatly increased the facilities of access to the Cemetery, while a wagonette is in constant readiness to convey visitors wherever they wish to go, on the payment of a small fee.

The beauty of the site, its advantageous situation in relation to the city, the taste and skill applied to the planting of the grounds, conforming to the natural surface so as to improve these and be improved by them, and the wise liberality of the management, have made Crown Hill Cemetery one of the finest in the country, and the pride of the Capital of the State.

ARTICLES OF ASSOCIATION.

SECTION 1. Under the laws of the State of Indiana, James Blake, Calvin Fletcher, Sr., James M. Ray, William H. Morrison, Thomas H. Sharpe, William O. Rockwood, William S. Hubbard, Theodore P. Haughey, Stoughton A. Fletcher, Jr., John C. New, Nicholas McCarty, Jesse D. Carmichael, Charles N. Todd, William Sheets, John M. Kitchen, Robert Browning, Addison L. Roache, George Tousey, Ovid Butler, J. H. Vajen, Elijah B. Martindale, Herman Lieber, William Wallace, Daniel Yandes, John M. Lord, John Armstrong, John Love, Almus E. Vinton, Thomas A. Morris and Jacob A. Crossland, agree to associate themselves, and they and their successors are hereby associated, as a body politic and perpetual corporation, under the name and title of the Crown Hill Cemetery, for providing within appropriate distance of the City of Indianapolis, in Marion County, Indiana, suitable grounds for the burial of the dead.

SEC. 2. The distinct and irrevocable principle on which this association is founded and to remain forever, except as is hereinafter allowed, is that the entire funds arising from the sale of burial lots, and the proceeds of any investment of said funds, shall be and they are specifically dedicated to the purchase and improvement of the grounds of the Cemetery, and keeping them durably and permanently enclosed and in perpetual repair through all future time, including all incidental expenses for approach to the Cemetery, and the proper management of the same; and that no part of such funds shall, as dividend, profit, or in any manner whatever, inure to the corporators.

SEC. 3. The said corporators shall, at least once in every year hereafter, fill, by election by ballot, all vacancies which may occur among them, and may, at the same time, or other times, increase and add to their number from those who may be lot-holders in the Cemetery, so that the said corporators shall never be reduced to less than fifteen nor exceed thirty members; but no power shall belong to any less number than fifteen to transact any other corporate business, except to fill vacancies of corporators; and they shall have power directly, or through their Board of Managers, to ordain and execute all such by-laws, not contrary to the Constitution and laws of the United States, or of this State, as may be needed for the government of the corporation, its officers, and affairs.

Provided, however, That any person holding title to a lot or any part thereof, whether by purchase, devise or inheritance, whether as joint tenants or tenants in common, shall be considered as a lot-holder within the meaning of this section, and qualified to be elected and act as corporator.

SEC. 4. The annual meeting of the corporators shall be held at such place in the City of Indianapolis, on the first Tuesday in the month of June, as of which notice shall be given ten days prior, by the Secretary, in two public newspapers of said city. In case of any failure to hold such annual meeting, at such date, within such month, and elect such Board of Managers, and fill any vacancies in the number of corporators, an election for such purposes, and doing any other business, may be had at a general meeting of the corporators at any other time, on ten days' notice being given by order of the Board of Managers, to be published as above; which order said Managers shall issue at the written request of any five of the corporators.

SEC. 5. The corporators shall, upon organizing and afterwards, at their annual meeting or general meeting when held, elect from their number, by ballot, seven Managers, who shall serve one year and until their successors are elected; and, in case of a vacancy occurring in such number, between the annual election by the corporators, the remaining Managers shall, by ballot, fill such vacancy.

SEC. 6. The said Managers shall have power to constitute themselves a Board by the appointment, of their own body, a President, whose duty it shall be to preside at their meetings, or, in his absence, any Manager then chosen may preside, and to sign all conveyances of lots or property conveyed by the corporation; and the Managers shall also appoint a Secretary and Treasurer, who shall each make a report of their proceedings, and the state of the finances, to the Board of Managers as often as may be required of them, and also at the annual meeting of the corporators. The Board of Managers, of whom five shall form a quorum, shall also have power to appoint a Superintendent, upon whom shall devolve, under its supervision, the general management of the Cemetery, and also all other officers, agents and workmen which may be needful, and to fix the compensation of all persons appointed by them, and the same discharge at pleasure ; to take from the Treasurer security for the faithful performance of his trust ; and the said Managers shall keep fair minutes of their acts and doings, and make a report thereof to the corporators at their annual meeting.

SEC. 7. The said Managers shall have power to contract for and purchase, from time to time, of the owner or owners thereof, as much land in Marion County, in this State, not exceeding six hundred acres, as they shall deem appropriate, permanently to provide a rural Cemetery, within six miles of the City of Indianapolis, as suitable grounds for the burial of the dead, and the same to lay out and ornament, and to divide and arrange into suitable plats and burial lots; remove and alter old and erect new buildings, have appropriate entrances and approaches made, and secure permanent enclosures, and to do all other things needful to be done to adapt the said grounds for the purposes of a Cemetery ; and to sell and convey said lots and burial lots, in fee simple or otherwise, for the purpose of sepulture, to individuals, societies, or congregations, without regard to sect, under such regulations as the said Managers may establish for the government of lot-holders, visitors to the Cemetery, and burial of the dead : *Provided*, That the lots granted by the said corporation for burial lots shall not be used for any other purpose. Said Managers may, in their discretion, at any time before disposing of the same for burial purposes, sell any portion of the lands purchased which may not be found appropriate to the object of the Cemetery, and purchase other suitable lands, not exceeding, finally, for the Cemetery, such six hundred acres. And, for the purpose of such purchase and acquiring such lands so to be used, or other needful expenditures of this corporation for carrying its indebtedness to the best advantage and affecting any of its objects, said Managers may borrow, on account of this association, any amount of money which they may deem to be requisite, and execute and deliver any needful obligation therefor, and may engage to pay interest not exceeding eight per cent. per annum thereon, and may give any needful lien on the property of the association, except that in that case it shall be provided expressly that whenever any section or portion of the grounds of the Cemetery be laid off, and ready for sale for burial use, the same as numbered and described on the plat of the Cemetery, shall be released from any and every such lien whatever, the Managers, if required, stipulating in such case that one-half of the proceeds of the sale of lots in such section laid off shall be applied to the discharge of the loan so secured by lien. The Board of Managers shall be authorized to invest any of the surplus funds, at any time, in the public securities of the United States of America, the City of Indianapolis, the State of Indiana, or any other State securities equally safe.

SEC. 8. Each corporator shall become a member of this association by subscribing these articles, and shall thereby be under obligation, at the request of the Treasurer of the corporation, to execute and deliver to him for the use of the Board of Managers, in effecting the object of this association, a note satisfactory to said Treasurer, payable at a bank in this city, without relief from valuation or appraisement laws, for the sum of five hundred dollars, in such installments thereof as may be called for, from time to time, by the Board of Managers, after ten days' written notice by the Secretary; which payment shall bear interest until they are repaid at the same rate as may be paid by the Board for any money that may be borrowed to purchase the real estate for the Cemetery; or such corporators or party giving such note may have credit for the amount of any such payment and such interest on any purchase of burial lots he may make in said Cemetery.

SEC. 9. Each corporator shall be entitled to one vote at any meeting of the corporators of this association.

SEC. 10. The seal of this corporation shall be of brass; an engraving thereon for an impression thereof shall be that of a broken column, enwreathed with ivy and evergreen, with the following words on its circle: "The Seal of the Crown Hill Cemetery."

SEC. 11. A failure to give the note which may as above be required of any corporator, when called upon by the Treasurer of the corporation, or to make any payment on such note after notice, when demanded, or a removal by any corporator from the County of Marion, Indiana, shall, *ipso facto*, vacate the membership of such corporator, and all his connection with this association shall thereupon cease.

SEC. 12. As no profit or income whatever can inure to the Managers or other corporators of this association, no individual liability whatever for its debts shall attach to them, or any of them, by its organization or its operations; and in all obligations which may be given by its Managers, as a Board or otherwise, on behalf of the association in its engagements, it shall be expressed or understood that no individual liability is thereby incurred by the Managers or corporators of the association, nor shall it ever be claimed thereon by the party or his assignee receiving such obligation.

SEC. 13. At any annual meeting of the corporators, duly notified, any alteration may be made in these Articles of Association by a vote of three-fourths of the whole corporators of the association, but no change shall ever be made in the distinct and irrevocable principle of the perpetuity of this association, and the dedication of all the net receipts thereof sufficiently to secure such perpetuity in the best manner to effect the objects of this association, according to the true tenor and meaning of these articles; but, after twenty-five years shall have expired from the organization of this corporation, by a vote of twenty-five of the corporators living within the County of Marion, Indiana, the Managers, after a fund has accumulated which will amply and permanently provide for the preservation, sustaining, and ornamenting the Cemetery, such alteration may be made, at any annual meeting, in the principles and limitations of these articles, as that out of the surplus funds of this Cemetery Association contributions and appropriations may be made by the Managers in aid of the poor of the City of Indianapolis.

SEC. 14. The Managers shall annually set apart not less than ten (10) per cent. of the gross annual receipts of the association for a fund which shall amply and permanently provide for the preservation, sustaining and ornamenting the Cemetery, and may annually set apart a larger per cent. of the receipts for such purpose, if in the judgment of the Managers it can be prudently done.

SEC. 15. The Managers may invest the funds of the association, not only in the way now provided by its articles, but also in good real estate mortgage securities: *Provided, however*, The real estate mortgaged shall be worth not less than twice the amount to be loaned.

In witness, whereof, the undersigned subscribe their names as corporators of this association, at Indianapolis, this twenty-fifth day of September, A. D. one thousand eight hundred and sixty-three.

JAMES BLAKE.	J. M. KITCHEN.
CALVIN FLETCHER, SR.	ROBERT BROWNING.
JAMES M. RAY.	A. L. ROACHE.
W. H. MORRISON.	GEORGE TOUSEY.
THOMAS H. SHARPE.	OVID BUTLER.
W. O. ROCKWOOD.	J. H. VAJEN.
WILLIAM S. HUBBARD.	E. B. MARTINDALE.
A. E. VINTON.	HERMAN LIEBER.
THEODORE P. HAUGHEY.	WILLIAM WALLACE.
STOUGHTON A. FLETCHER, JR.	DANIEL YANDES.
JOHN C. NEW.	J. M. LORD.
NICHOLAS MCCARTY.	J. A. CROSSLAND.
JESSE D. CARMICHAEL.	T. A. MORRIS.
CHARLES N. TODD.	JOHN LOVE.
WILLIAM SHEETS.	JOHN ARMSTRONG.

JAMES M. RAY, *President.*
THEO. P. HAUGHEY, *Secretary.*

RULES AND REGULATIONS.

Regulations Concerning Visitors.

THE Secretary will issue to each proprietor of one or more lots one ticket of admission into the Cemetery under the following regulations, and such as may hereafter be adopted, the violation of any of which, or the loan of the ticket, will involve a forfeiture of the privilege:

1. Tickets, to be styled "Special Tickets," may be issued to persons not proprietors, some members of whose families may have been interred on a "single interment" lot or on the lot of a proprietor.

2. All proprietors of lots are requested to present their tickets of admission at the gate before entering the grounds.

3. All visitors, whether in vehicles or on foot, are required to have tickets, to be presented to the gate-keeper, in order to gain admittance. Such tickets can be obtained on application to the Superintendent, at the office of the association, or of the President or any of the Managers.

4. Each proprietor shall have the privilege of introducing strangers.

5. No riding or driving will be allowed through the grounds faster than a walk or slow trot.

6. Horses must not be left, unless fastened where places are provided for the purpose; and no bicycle riding or riding on horseback will be permitted on the grounds.

7. All persons are prohibited from writing upon, defacing or injuring any monument or other structure, in or belonging to the Cemetery.

8. No flowers, shrubs or plants to be taken out of the Cemetery grounds by any one under any circumstances.

9. All persons are prohibited from plucking any flower, either wild or cultivated, injuring or breaking any tree, shrub or plant, or entering on any individual lot without leave.

10. All persons are prohibited from discharging firearms in the Cemetery, except for military interments.

11. The gates are opened at sunrise and closed at sunset.

12. No money may be paid to the keeper of the gate, or any other person in the employ of the Cemetery, in reward for any personal services or attention.

13. Children will not be admitted unless attended by some person who will be responsible for their conduct.

14. No persons having refreshments of any kind will be permitted to bring them within the grounds, nor will any smoking be allowed.

15. Persons having baskets, or any like article, must leave them in charge of the gate-keeper.

16. Visitors are reminded that these grounds are sacredly devoted to the interment of the dead, and that a strict observance of the decorum which should characterize such a place will be required.

17. Any person disturbing the quiet and good order of the place by noise or other improper conduct, or who shall violate any of the foregoing rules, will be compelled instantly to leave the grounds.

18. Dogs will not be admitted in the inclosure.

19. No omnibus will be admitted within the grounds.

20. The Superintendent is charged with the execution of these rules and regulations. It is of the utmost importance that there should be a strict observance of all the proprieties due the place, whether embraced in these regulations or not, as no impropriety will be permitted to pass unnoticed. All well-disposed persons will confer a favor by informing the Superintendent of any breach of these rules that may come under their notice.

REGULATIONS GOVERNING THE PURCHASE OF LOTS.

Persons desiring to acquire lots in the Cemetery, and not being able to pay the entire price thereof in cash, will be required to pay not less than one-third of the price in cash, and to execute his note or notes for the remainder of the price in such amounts and upon such time as may be mutually agreed upon. But the payment of such money and the execution of such note or notes shall not confer any title whatsoever upon the purchaser to said lot or any part thereof until all of said notes shall have been fully paid. And upon failure to pay any of said notes in whole or in part at maturity, the Cemetery shall have the right at any time thereafter to enter upon said lot and remove any body or bodies interred thereon, together with all monuments or marking stones, to other grounds reserved for single interments; and in such event, all moneys theretofore paid shall be deemed and taken as having been paid in consideration of the right to bury upon such lot and the occupancy thereof for the time being, and for the price of said grounds to which such body or bodies shall have been transferred, and to cover the cost of transferring such remains, monuments and marking stones; and thereafter such proposed purchasers shall have no right or equity whatever in the lands so conditionally purchased. And in no case shall a deed be executed for any lot until the same has been fully paid for.

RULES AND REGULATIONS PRESCRIBING THE CONDITIONS, LIMITATIONS AND PRIVILEGES TO WHICH EVERY LOT IN CROWN HILL CEMETERY IS SUBJECT.

1. The proprietor of each lot shall have the right to erect proper stones, monuments or sepulchral structures, strictly subject to the regulations governing the same.

2. The proprietor of each lot shall erect, at his or her expense, suitable landmarks of stone, at the corners or boundaries thereof, not less than two and one-half feet long, and set even with the surface of the ground, and shall also cause the number thereof to be legibly and permanently marked on one of such stones; and if the proprietor shall omit, for thirty days after notice, to erect such landmarks and mark the number, the Managers shall have the authority to cause the same to be done at the expense of the proprietor.

3. All persons are prohibited from planting trees, shrubs or plants on lots or graves, and on and after November 1, 1894, will be prohibited from planting any flowers in the Cemetery grounds. Flowers are permitted in vases or urns, and cut flowers may be placed upon the graves, but will be removed as soon as they become faded and unsightly in appearance.

4. If any trees or shrubs situated in any lot shall, by means of their roots, branches, height, or otherwise, become detrimental to the adjacent lots, walks or

LOOKING WEST FROM MAIN ENTRANCE.

avenues, or dangerous or inconvenient to passengers, it shall be the duty of the Managers, and they have the right, to enter into the said lot and remove the said trees or shrubs or such parts thereof as are thus detrimental, dangerous or inconvenient.

5. All lots set with grass or sodded, and not unnecessarily encumbered with shrubbery, or otherwise, will be kept in order free of expense to the owner.

6. Lots shall not be used for any other purpose than as a place of burial for the dead; and no trees within the lots or borders shall be cut down or destroyed without the consent of the Managers of the corporation.

7. If any monument, effigy, or other structure whatever, or any inscription be placed in or upon any lot, which shall be determined by the major part of the Managers to be offensive or improper, or injurious to the appearance of the surrounding lots or grounds, the said Managers shall have the right, and it shall be their duty, to enter upon such lot and remove the said offensive or improper object or objects.

8. Proprietors shall not allow interments to be made in their lots for a remuneration. All interments in lots shall be restricted to the members of the family and relations of the proprietor thereof, except special permission to the contrary be obtained, in writing, from the Superintendent.

9. All deeds when executed shall be construed as simply granting to the proprietor of the lot conveyed the right to use said lot for burial purposes, for the interment of himself, his family, his relations and descendants, and such other persons as he shall have the permission of the Superintendent to bury thereon as above provided. But such burial right shall be personal to himself and the persons above named; and such right shall not be transferable, either by voluntary or involuntary conveyance, to any other person or persons without the express consent of the Board of Managers of the Cemetery.

10. All lot-owners are prohibited from selling their lots in whole or in part, or from transferring the same without the express consent of the Board of Managers of the Cemetery.

11. Private fences or enclosures around lots will not be allowed.

12. No interments are allowed until the payment for the lot is provided for, as required by the regulations prescribed for the purchase of lots; and if at any time any note or notes, executed upon the execution of a conditional contract for the purchase of a lot, shall be past due, no further interment shall be allowed thereon until such note or notes shall either be paid or the prompt payment thereof secured to the satisfaction of the Board of Managers.

13. All graves shall be dug by workmen in the employment of the corporation, for which reasonable charges will be made.

14. Proprietors wishing improvements on their lots must pay for the same to the Superintendent when ordered.

15. Trellises of any kind are prohibited on the grounds of the Cemetery.

16. No enclosures of any kind allowed around graves.

17. No trees, plants or shrubs in the corners of lots as boundary marks allowed.

18. All graves to be sodded all over, the mounds to be four inches in height in the center, with rounded sides and ends. All graves to be made, sodded and cared for by the Cemetery Company.

19. Lot owners are prohibited from placing on lots or graves all toys, cases, boxes, globes, shells, cans, jugs, bottles and bric-a-brac of every description; any such articles found on the Cemetery grounds will be removed.

20. No wooden benches, chairs, settees, head-boards or wooden articles of any kind allowed on the grounds.

21. Heavy loads will not be allowed to enter, unless by permission of the Superintendent.

22. The grading of all lots must be under the direction of the Superintendent, and by hands employed regularly on the grounds.

MONUMENTAL WORK.

1. All monumental work must be brought into the Cemetery grounds at the east entrance.

2. All foundations for all stone work must be built by the Cemetery Company, and must be ordered and paid for at the Superintendent's office at least two weeks in advance of the arrival of the work.

3. All monuments and head-stones must be of a good quality of granite, marble or other stone adapted to such purposes. No other material will be allowed in the Cemetery grounds.

4. No head or foot-stones over one foot in height above the surface of the lot allowed, and must be four inches or more in thickness.

5. Only one stone can be placed at a grave; both head and foot-stones not allowed.

6. At the single interments no monument or stone of any kind over one foot in height will be allowed, and must be placed at the head of the grave.

7. Curbings of stone around graves will not be allowed on the Cemetery grounds.

8. Only one monument on a lot will be allowed, except by permission of the Board of Managers.

9. Vaults or tombs are not recommended, but will be permitted, provided the plans for same are approved by the Superintendent, to whom they must be in all cases submitted before the work is begun.

10. In the erection of monuments, vaults, tombs or other structures, a place will be designated by the Superintendent for the deposit of the stones, brick or other materials, which shall not remain longer on the ground than is actually necessary for their construction.

11. All workmen employed in the construction of vaults, erection of monuments, landmarks, or any other work, must be subject to the control and direction of the Superintendent; and any workman failing to conform to this regulation will not be permitted afterward to work on the grounds.

LIST OF LOT-HOLDERS.

OWNERS' NAMES.	Lot No.	Section
Adams, W. L. ...	26	12
Allan, James	30	16
Adams, Henry C	59	16
Abrams, John	66	16
Aldag, Charles	65	19
Aldag, August .... part of	30	21
Adams, Wesley M	72	27
Altland, Samuel T	58	27
Armacost, Mary E	93	31
Altland, Hiram .... part of	216	25
Aldag, Louis	286	31
Adams, George F	88	14
Adam, William	222	31
Arndt, Charles H	211	18
Allman, Haman	30	33
Abrams, Benjamin F	324	32
Andra, Wilhelmina	38	34
Adams, Elizabeth B	12	34
Altman, Wilhelmina	339	32
Adams, Samuel C .... part of	26	1
Adams, L. F .... part of	4	3
Adams, W. H .... part of	397	32
Adams, Vilete .... part of	77	37
Adams, Henry C .... part of	66	16
Adams, Hannah V .... part of	25	33
Artman, William A	223	30

OWNERS' NAMES.	Lot No.	Section
Ampt, Herman	184	39
Adams, Ida M .... part of	66	19
Adams, Margaret .... part of	176	39
Achey, Mrs. Mary	6 and 7	5
Allen, William	52	1
Anderson, George P	34	7
Averill, Joseph	97	4
Alexander, George W	34	4
Armentrout, G. W .... part of	12	12
Abbett, Lawson	85	2
Anderson, Julia A. P .... part of	19	12
Aneshaensel, Charles	47	17
Abrecht, August	20	17
Apperson, Chas. M .... part of	28	17
Alexander, William	36	12
Applegate, Margaret	50	21
Avery, E. O	110	25
Allen, Geo. W	83	25
Albrecht, George A	55	25
Abbett, Charles H	32	14
Anderson, David	15	27
Allen, H. R	23	23
Allred, Mrs. Fanny	239	31
Avery, John L. and John P	9	2
Avery, Hardress	272	32
Avery, Melville D	273	32
Anderson, J. E	82	32
Aebker, C. Henry	214	32
Anderson, Laura	2	18
Albersmeier, William	55	33
Armentrout, George and Ella	16	33
Aker, Charlotte E	252	18
Anther, Kate L	181	34
Anderson, George .... part of	233	25
Armstead, Louella	281	18
Anderson, Stella .... part of	182	16
Alexander, Gideon .... sub. 6	58	20
Anderson, Marcellus S	12	35

1397233

CROWN HILL CEMETERY.

OWNERS' NAMES.	Lot No.	Section
Ackelow, Herman .... part of	37	35
Asche, Mary	63	35
Ahrens, William .... part of	226	35
Ashmead, John	41	16
Andrews, John B	61	4
Albrecht, Maurice J .... part of	82	33
Anderson, Aquilla	172	38
Angelo, Alonzo E .... part of	87	36
Anderson, John H	368	38
Allfree, James B	106	37
Albersmeier, Henry	337	38
Alexander, Samuel B	137	37
Ashley, Thomas	328	38
Algeo, John	53	39
Allen, Cyrus and Isaac	233	37
Allen, Anna	121	25
Abercrombie, Laura M .... part of	355	38
Anderson, Alma H .... part of	18	33
Allen, John R	141	36
Albrecht, Louisa .... part of	392	38
Allen, Sarah M .... part of	408	37
Anderegg, John A .... part of	81	39
Anderson, Leman C	255	37
Aebker, Mary	458	39
Atkins, E. C	20	6
Allison, Joseph E .... part of	80	15
Atkinson, Thomas .... part of	138	16
Ainsworth, Francis B .... part of	170	25
Atkinson, Benjamin	119	31
Aldrich, Alexander W	103	31
Aldridge, Hester Ann .... part of	2	3
Allridge, A. and C .... part of	70	2
Austmillar, William	103	34
Allgire, Mary A	342	32
Allison, John F	285	18
Atkins, E. C. & Co	169	33
Adkisson, Elizabeth W .... part of	31	35
Adkisson, John C .... part of	32	35

OWNERS' NAMES.	Lot No.	Section
Allison, Mrs. Belle T	91	35
Aldrich, John D	133	36
Aichhorn, Christian F	38	38
Allison, Myra J .... part of	38	36
Albright, Michael .... part of	87	36
Aldrich, Ella .... part of	30	20
Allinder, Sallie	76	36
Aichhorn, Sophia	282	38
Achgill, Anthony .... part of	66	33
Atkins, Adelaide G	48	36
Amick, George L. and Eliza A	185	39
Aldrich, David E	455	39
Aitken, David L	386	37
Armstrong, John	10, 23, 24	5
Alford, Thomas G .... part of	27	7
Alvord, E. S	16	11
Armstrong, Henry	1 and 2	19
Alhand, John L .... part of	23	17
Amos, Thomas D .... part of	45	19
Amthor, William L	29	9
Aston George	73	21
Athon, James S., estate of	49	13
Armstrong, William	59	25
Armstrong, Isaiah J .... part of	134	27
Arnold, Emma	35	2
Arnold, John	234	32
Arnold Samuel	219	18
Anthony, Sarah M	280	18
Arnold, Sarah A .... part of	178	4
Almond, Enos A	108	33
Amos, Mrs. Lydia	287	35
Armstrong, Robert B	140	38
Arnold, William M	180	38
Albro, Orville H .... part of	20	2
Alford, William E	2	37
Armstrong, Carrie .... part of	298	38
Armstrong, Washington	191	31
Abromet, Elizabeth	47	36

OWNERS' NAMES.

Name		Lot No.	Section
Armstrong, William S	part of	16 and 17	25
Armstrong, William J		335	39
Alford, Cora		266	37
Austin, George T		138	2
Arthur, Thomas		195	16
Aufderheide, Henry		107	16
Angus, W. W		71	17
Ault, Elizabeth C		197	25
Arbuckle, Matthew		7	31
Aubrey, Martha		257	31
Asmus, Elizabeth		214	31
Andrus, Rev. Dr. Reuben		199	34
Anschuetz, Gustave and Edward		199	35
Ault, Alfred C		154	38
Arthurs, William	part of	27	9
Arthur, Elizabeth		195	37
Aufderheide, William		70	39
Augstein, Charles T	part of	516	39
Ayres, Levi		140	2
Ayres, Lyman S		19	11
Ayers, Richard		13	39
Bramwell, John M		3 and 4	1
Bavington, Albert	part of	35	5
Blane, Mrs. J. D		148	2
Bacon, Hiram		43	3
Baker, Abraham H		27	2
Braden, William		19	6
Blake, James		69	1
Blake, Charles		87	2
Barnes, Eunice	part of	90	2
Bates, Hervey		1	8
Bradley and Kitchen		29 and 30	6
Barbour, Lucian		74 and 75	5
Bacon, Deborah	part of	135	2
Barry, E. H		35	7
Bassett, Mrs. Amanda		16	5
Barker, Myron J		24	11
Baker, Frederick		16	1

OWNERS' NAMES.	Lot No.	Section
Bradshaw, James M	51	13
Barnes, Albert A	43	1
Basey, Mrs. Elizabeth	82	4
Bradley, Jeptha W	43	16
Barth, Amanda	12	16
Barneclo, Rebecca	58 and 59	16
Black, Mrs. Rachel	11	16
Batty, John H .... part of	81	15
Balls, Antoine .... part of	5	4
Barker, Mrs. Lucinda	123	16
Bals, Charles H. G	39	3
Black, G. H .... part of	148	16
Baird, William	72	16
Baoking, Frederick	144	16
Baker, Mrs. Sarah J	34	16
Balz, Peter, Philip and Fred	33	3
Ballweg, Ambrose	60	17
Base, Ernest	55	17
Bailey, George W	37	17
Baster, Edward .... part of	29	17
Braden, Fannie D	39	14
Bradshaw, William A .... part of	8	13
Baggs, Frederick .... part of	38	12
Banse, William .... part of	38	20
Barret, E. G	45	20
Blair, John .... part of	10	9
Branham, Edward	90	14
Barbee, Robert B .... part of	27	13
Blauvelt, John H	47	21
Barbee, Samson, Sr., estate .... part of	27	13
Barrol, Frankie Mabel	73	25
Blank, Anton	138 and 139	25
Bauer, Henry .... part of	105	25
Bramkamp, Elizabeth .... part of	11	25
Balls, Chas. H .... part of	48	21
Ballinger, Charles	134	25
Baine, William	55	27
Bray, Margaret	41	31

CROWN HILL CEMETERY.

OWNERS' NAMES.	Lot No.	Section
Banke, John Henry	86	27
Branson, Mrs. Anna E.	11	22
Bradshaw, Mrs. Margaret .... part of	58	13
Bradymier, Christian C	6	31
Blake, John .... part of	25	1
Bagby, Charlotte F.	143	27
Balfour, James	106	31
Back, Mrs. Frederica	240	31
Bradley, Homer .... part of	243	31
Bassett, Thomas M .... part of	64	13
Bray, Mary E	273	31
Bradley, William B	271	31
Black, Charles H .... part of	185	25
Brandenburg, Charles A	205	31
Brake, Nancy A .... part of	223	31
Barth, John W	20	32
Bauer, Jacob and Louisa	209	31
Barnhill, Robert .... part of	178	32
Blake, Fred .... part of	244	25
Braidhoft, Louis	43	32
Baxter, Edmund .... part of	26	19
Baxter, Buonaparte .... part of	26	19
Baker, Albert R .... part of	21	23
Bailie, Hamilton	305	32
Bazel, Evaline	7	20
Bacon, Frank M. and Mary E	154	32
Backus, Victor M .... part of	177	27
Barnard, Eugene E .... part of	65	13
Ballantyne, William	140	32
Barrett, Simpson K .... part of	204	18
Brake, Mrs. Ida and Thomas	60	33
Baggerly, Chas. W .... part of	255	25
Bradley, Wilhelmina D	195	32
Barbour, Harriet	95	33
Basey, Frederick	57	33
Brattain, Mary E	311	32
Blackledge, Susan K .... part of	106	27
Barekdall, Mary	48	33

Owners' Names.	Lot No.	Section
Bartlett, John William	100 and 101	18
Black, Jerry	111	18
Baumer, John	99	34
Baird, Mrs. Ella	117	18
Black, William M	330	32
Barnhizer, Mrs. Sallie	26	34
Bailey, Anna E	277	18
Bainake, Mary	129	18
Baker, William L	365	32
Barlosius, Theresia	139	34
Baker, Midie J	104	34
Barnes, George W	112	34
Bartholomew, Pliny W., Harris M. and Sarah B.	5	34
Bailie, Robert .... part of	109	33
Barclay, Isabella .... part of	57	27
Bacon, Robert D .... part of	363	32
Black, George W	314	18
Baker, James P. and Mary R. P ...... part of	240	25
Baker, William H .... part of	89	27
Ballard, William .... sub 1	85	20
Bailiff, Daniel W .... sub 6	25	20
Baker, Elizabeth .... sub 12	58	20
Baldwin, Silas	103	14
Baker, Mary	21	35
Bates, Katie	161	33
Brady, John .... part of	168	32
Bradley, Leland J .... part of	17	35
Brattain, Amanda E	354	32
Baker, Julia A	358	35
Ballweg, Fred .... part of	37	35
Brattain, Wilhelmina P	99	35
Baird, Mrs. Jeannette .... part of	72	17
Blaich, Gottleib F	116	35
Braxton, Mary Alice	139	35
Barrow, George and Charles A	137	35
Braendlein, Henry .... part of	314	35
Baron, George M. and John G	166	35
Baker, Joel A	180	35

OWNERS' NAMES.	Lot No.	Section
Bass, William Harrison	211	35
Barnett, Thomas, Sr., heirs of .... part of	235	25
Barneclo, Wilber G .... part of	36	36
Ballard, Mrs. Florence .... part of	86	20
Baggs, Chas. A .... part of	81	33
Bauer, Conrad	161	32
Barthel, Albert .... part of	160	32
Bakemeier, Mary C	63	38
Baptist, John Henry	73	38
Brandt, Herman T	70	15
Bade, Henry C	107	38
Brandenburger, Elizabeth	332	35
Black, Jennie M .... part of	5	20
Baley, Simon T	87	36
Blackshaw, Anna .... part of	57	14
Baron, Henry H. .... part of	189	38
Bauer, Louis G .... part of	366	38
Braden, Robert B.	77	21
Barr, Mary H	91	34
Baughman, Herschel R. A. and Kate G	99	36
Baker, Kate	214	36
Baur, Richard	146	37
Brandes, Herman	287	38
Bailey, Leon O .... part of	119	2
Brackin, Thomas E	155 and 156	4
Barkley, James	279	31
Barnes, George H .... part of	111	38
Bragg, Stokeley S.	143	39
Baker, Dorus J .... part of	103	27
Bartlett, William H .... part of	226	39
Bates, Elizabeth C	153	39
Black, John A	140	36
Barnhart, Alice B .... part of	89	39
Baine, Thomas W	221	37
Baaske, Charles T .... part of	220	39
Bradley, John	90	39
Baker, Millidge A	418	39
Baldwin, Isaac D	137	36

CROWN HILL CEMETERY.

OWNERS' NAMES.	Lot No.	Section
Barker, Charles S.	162	39
Barratt, John M.	275	37
Ballmann, John Heury	250	39
Baker, Mrs. Bertha	119	39
Bradley, Giles S	301	32
Bader, Elizabeth	488	39
Barth, Jacob S	268	37
Bakemeyer, Henry C	188	39
Bartol, Harry B	328	37
Bauer, George, Mary and Elizabeth	103	39
Blair, Jesse H........ part of	206	36
Benton, A. R	30	5
Brenninger, Augustus	169	4
Beck, Edward	88	2
Bechert, John	141	2
Bernauer, Joseph	64	4
Beeler, Fielding........ part of	3	6
Brewster, Mrs. Sarah A........ part of	60	3
Bender, Mrs. Jemima and heirs	187	16
Berry, D. M	106	15
Beal, Joshua........ part of	86	15
Bell, Miletus	22	17
Beyer, Henry	76	17
Beall, Mrs. Elizabeth........ part of	101	15
Becker, Jacob	61	15
Berk, Martin	24	15
Benson, John A........ part of	81	20
Berryman, William	66	21
Bernhard, Ernst........ part of	49	15
Bergener, G........ part of	65	15
Beinburg, Casper	15	9
Beltz, Jacob........ part of	20	9
Beck, Conrad	3	25
Benton, Isaac S........ part of	51	15
Berns, John........ part of	146	25
Bermann, Henry and Louis	92	16
Brester, William........ part of	129	25
Bennett, A. L.	2	27

OWNERS' NAMES.	Lot No.	Section
Berk, Annie ... part of	49	27
Becker, Emilie	140	27
Belck, Frederick	184	25
Bernhard, John	241	31
Becker, Joseph	132	27
Beever, J. R. and J. E ... part of	3	3
Bell, Dr. Guido	327	31
Brester, John	274	31
Beymer, Webster	1	32
Benson, John S.	199	32
Berner, Frederick ... part of	43	17
Bein, C. F.	280	31
Berryman, James M	78	32
Beerbower, Matilda L.	202	32
Belman, Virginia	51	18
Bennett, J. Wesley ... part of	151	18
Beck, Fred	153	32
Bennerscheidt, August ... part of	49 and 54	18
Bethune, Norman W	26	33
Bea, Charles	162	16
Becklay, George Washington	230	18
Beard, Rev. J. N	228	31
Bence, Robert and Caroline ... part of	136	27
Belck, Henry ... part of	97	34
Beam, Mary H	207	34
Bernd, Peter	311	18
Beyrsdorfer, Mattie ... part of	341	31
Beyer, Frederick G ... part of	112	33
Beam, George W ... part of	155	27
Berdel, Barbara	70	35
Beckman, William C	156	35
Bremer, John D. and Frederick	44	35
Becklay, Martha	24	37
Beville, Henry H	101	35
Behrens, Henry and William ... part of	316	31
Beck, Albert T ... part of	36	6
Bergundthal, David C	97	35
Breyer, Margaret ... part of	16	35

CROWN HILL CEMETERY.

OWNERS' NAMES. Lot No. Section

Name		Lot No.	Section
Bennett, William	part of	61	35
Brewin, Annie E.	part of	252	35
Bennett, Horace T		23	15
Breil, John H		288	35
Beall, Balcom		32	38
Bennett, Montague G	part of	34	38
Beard, John M		173	35
Beermann, Henry		7	38
Berndt, John G		336	35
Beachman, Sarah L	part of	171	38
Beerman, August		200	38
Beck, Conrad	part of	111	27
Bergmann, Caroline E		216	38
Berg, Henrietta	part of	384	38
Bertermann, John		63	36
Berner, Gottlieb	part of	366	38
Behymer, Omer T		5	37
Bennett, Catharine and Jas. E	part of	322	38
Bevan, John		132	37
Bennett, Margaret J		198	38
Berg, John		120	37
Brewer, Alfred and Calvin L		138	36
Benner Arthur		309	38
Brehmer, John J	part of	27	36
Bertelsmann, Henry and Charles		115	39
Bretney, Eugene		150	36
Beisenherz, Henry D		355	39
Beltz, Frank P	part of	189	25
Bernd, Daniel		338	39
Bernloehr, John		109	39
Bellis, John R		217	39
Bender, Conrad	part of	382	39
Beaning, William	part of	382	39
Beans, Mary E		287	37
Benson, Margaret A	part of	91	37
Beveridge, Albert J	part of	76	14
Beatty, Albert J	part of	496	39
Billingsley, A. D		29	2

OWNERS' NAMES.	Lot No.	Section
Briggs, Wm. G .... part of	177	4
Bisbing, Jacob J	38	1
Bingham, Joseph J	69	14
Bingham, Joseph J	111	4
Bigelow, J. S	81	5
Birchard, Emily	72	2
Bliss, Eleazer	102	2
Bright, R. J	20	14
Bingham, W. P .... part of	22	7
Biehler, George and John...	169	16
Bishop, George M	15	19
Birrer, Mary A .... part of	159	25
Binager, George T .... part of	170	25
Birch, James .... part of	30	27
Britton, John	105	31
Birge, James A	21	31
Bristor, Esther A	221	25
Bidleman, Winslow R	29	25
Bixby, June M .... part of	191	25
Brinker, August .... part of	287	31
Bieler, Jacob L	291	31
Brinkmeyer, George H	47, 48, 55, 56	18
Bridges, Charles W .... part of	255	25
Brinkmeyer, Mrs. Charlotte .... part of	131	27
Bischoff, Charles	290	18
Biggers, Mary C	103	18
Bridenbaugh, Annie E	262	18
Bigelow, Eliza	81	34
Beidenmeister, Charles A	124	33
Blinn, Edward W	170	33
Britton, Charles O .... sub 13	58	20
Billmire, Rachel .... sub 5	85	20
Billing, Gustave	221	35
Billingsley, D. F	234	35
Britton, Mary A .... part of	65	35
Bishop, Louis	78	38
Bird, Mary C .... part of	66	38
Brill, John C	139	38

OWNERS' NAMES.	Lot No.	Section
Bilger, Grace	383	38
Bishop, Clara ... part of	167	38
Bright, Mattie	26	37
Briggs, Mary H ... part of	13	36
Brinkman, William	4	37
Binckley, Martha E	23	31
Biegler, Portia	40	39
Bicknell, Ernest P	584	39
Birchfield, James W ... part of	186	18
Biddinger, James H	254	37
Bird, William C	289	37
Bigger, Richard Frederick ... part of	47	14
Bistline, Arvilla M	443	37
Brown, James W	35	1
Brown, Mrs. Julia A	30 and 32	2
Boring, Ephraim	108	4
Brown, R. T	110	4
Brown, John William	43	5
Boaz, Mrs. N. J ... part of	6	7
Browning, Robert	2	7
Browning, J. W ... part of	7	1
Brownlee, Samuel	101	4
Bobbs, Mrs. Catharine C	53	7
Bowen, Silas T	12 and 19	8
Brown, Austin H. and George	55	5
Brown, John	73	4
Brown, Ellison	6	16
Brown, Theresa M	89	16
Brown, James H	153	16
Boerum, J. S ... part of	62	3
Boaz, Naomi J ... part of	3	3
Brown, William J	64	16
Browning, Edmund ... part of	5	7
Brouse, J. A ... part of	3	5
Brown, Jeremiah	70	16
Bouchet, Sophia	59	17
Bose, Mrs. Henrietta	14	17
Bock, Christian	128	16

A WINTER SCENE.

OWNERS' NAMES.	Lot No.	Section
Brooke, Gilbert M.	71	14
Brown, John M	37	15
Bossert, John	74	17
Bomgardner, Emily	6	19
Broecking, Ernst	60	19
Brown, Peter D	76	15
Bond, Fred........ part of	23	20
Boecksmith, Henry	22	20
Boecher, Henry........ part of	46	16
Bomgardner, Isaac	57	20
Brown, Hiram........ part of	62	7
Brown, George H........ part of	34	19
Brodamier, Ann C	92	15
Borgmann, Fred........ part of	87	19
Bowser, Henry	24	3
Boetticher, Otto	67	21
Boyd, L. A.	37	25
Brock, Thomas........ part of	7	15
Brown, James D........ part of	155	25
Bolser, Charles H	131	25
Brown, Rev'd Joseph	69	21
Brown, Obediah and John H. F	162	25
Borst, Margaret	161	25
Bowen, George	38	27
Bombarger, David	75	31
Bombarger, J. E	76	31
Brouse, Andrew	170	27
Boley, S. M	130	31
Bohlen, D. A	175	25
Bowersmith, Charles E	60	31
Bohne, Henry	206	25
Brock, Robert	68	27
Brown, James G	153	27
Boatwright, William........ part of	256	25
Bowyer, Anna	112	32
Boyce, C. G	70	32
Brown, Edgar A	178	27
Bowles, George W	182	32

OWNERS' NAMES.	Lot No.	Section
Borchert, Clara W................................	292	32
Boyer, Alice....................... part of	147	2
Boswell, Joseph E................. part of	245	31
Boyer, James A.................................	141	32
Brooks, M. Henry................. part of	151	18
Borncamp, William.............................	193	18
Brown, Lucretia M................ part of	280	32
Brown, Anna M.................... part of	2	15
Brown, John W.................................	97	33
Bloomer, Susan.................................	96	33
Bosley, Mrs. Mary M...........................	215	18
Bollinger, James................................	135	4
Bockstahler, Sophia.............. part of	169	32
Bockstahler, Minnie............. part of	169	32
Boaz, Charles G. and Burling..................	303	31
Bowser, Levi C..................................	188	34
Bottome, Free A................................	145	34
Bowman, John H..............................	301	18
Bottler, Julius...................................	330	35
Browning, Frank................. part of	22	35
Boketoh, Ada..................... sub 4	85	20
Bowen, Lucinda Jane...........................	108	35
Brown, Frank M.................. part of	72	3
Bodine, James E................................	192	35
Boyce, William H................. part of	79	14
Boutwell, George...............................	258	35
Brooks, Maria.................... part of	61	35
Boese, Henry C.................................	79	35
Boyd, David M.................................	106	14
Boyd, Francis...................................	59	38
Bodenmiller, Leonard............ part of	41	38
Brown, Minnie................... part of	77	38
Brown, Maria.................... part of	87	20
Bonzheim, Regina..............................	27	27
Brown, Mary A.................................	78	37
Bookwalter, Sarah A............. part of	3	17
Brown, Helena C...............................	375	38
Bowen, Adaline C...............................	205	38

OWNERS' NAMES.

Owner		Lot No.	Section
Brooks, John and John W		381	38
Brown, Charles H. and Donnell M	part of	369	38
Boyer, Emma		86	37
Bloom, Elizabeth		81	36
Boynton, Charles S	part of	255	35
Brown, Joseph F		134	37
Bogert, Ralph E	part of	121	37
Bobbs, William C	part of	252	25
Bowes, Henry J		71	19
Brown, Garret A	part of	288	38
Brown, Albert G		6	39
Brouse, Charles W	part of	41	7
Board of Children's Guardians		141	37
Booth, Louisa		197	37
Bohn, Julia		228	36
Boller, Peter		249	37
Boese, Christian H		191	37
Bosthofer, Amelia A	part of	177	39
Bowman, George W	part of	76	39
Boeling, Ferdinand		175	39
Brown, Lucy	part of	201	36
Boyd, James M	part of	155	27
Bowman, Frederick W		208	37
Bloom, George H		150	39
Brown, Nathaniel J	part of	181	39
Bowman, Ida M	part of	219	39
Brown, Marcus L		254	36
Bowser, Jacob and Jennie		279	39
Brown, John F	part of	379	38
Born, John		492	39
Boyle, Henry J	part of	266	18
Bowers, Albert A		354	37
Brochhausen, Annie M		421	39
Brown, Walter S	part of	267	38
Bone, William M	part of	197	39
Booth, Caroline		265	37
Bown, Phillip C		403	37
Boettcher, Fred		425	39

OWNERS' NAMES.	Lot No.	Section
Boggess, Henry H............................part of	73	5
Bullard, Mrs. Kate	34	1
Buckmar, Mrs. M. W...............................	12	4
Blue, Elias and Garret.............................	20	5
Butler, Ovid	13, 14, 17, 18	6
Bruener, Elizabeth	18	4
Burk, John and Helen M........................	17	5
Burkhart, Mrs. Susan..............................	97	2
Bunte, John B., heirs of.........................	80	3
Blue, Benjamin.......................................	34	12
Buchter, George.....................................	57	16
Bruce, George ....part of	104	2
Burk, Sylvertus L....................................	40	16
Burford, Miles W....................................	68	14
Buchrig, Mrs. Rebecca...........................	77	16
Bulach, Anton	159	16
Burnam, Henry C...................................	6	17
Bruning, Frederick......................part of	83	16
Budd, John R..	97	16
Butsch, Cynthia Ann	69	15
Butler, Margaret S ....part of	158	31
Buchanan, Catherine	216	25
Buschmann, William	24	14
Bullock, James B. and Melinda .....part of	24	23
Butt, Fredericka	20	31
Brunson, H. C..	107	31
Burus, Harry G., Robert P. and Loura B .....part of	300	31
Brunner, Caroline	244	32
Bullock, Onslow L	50	32
Bruening, John F	249	31
Burgan, J. C..	77	32
Butler, John M...........................part of	65	13
Buscher, William....................................	109	18
Burnes, Mrs. J. E	190	18
Busch, George C	65	18
Butsch, Mary...	70	33
Bruce, George W.......................part of	67	16
Brundage, Reuben N	91	18

OWNERS' NAMES.	Lot No.	Section
Buchanan, John C.	106	18
Burton, George H	142	31
Bushnell, Daniel W.	243	18
Burke, Mrs. Mary C.	81	18
Burnes, Sarah W.	329	32
Buchhorn, Sophia L	28	34
Burke, Mrs. Mary	148	34
Burris, William Edward	114	34
Brueickner, Christian Fred	55	34
Bush, George	120	34
Burkert, William O	149	34
Bruce, James P.	201	34
Bush, Zachariah ... part of	229	25
Butz, J. W	310	32
Bruce, Ida B ... part of	204	34
Butterworth, Charles	146	33
Burgess, Hannah	107	35
Burton, Martin ... part of	383	32
Bruhn, August ... part of	335	35
Buck, John W	310	35
Brush, John T	386	32
Blume, Julia	145	35
Burton, James M	121	35
Bruschker, Netta Fasi ... part of	250	31
Burns, Elizabeth	120	35
Bruce, John J. and Martha M	76	35
Burkhardt, Daniel B	220	35
Bussey, Beulah A	256	35
Bruner, Jacob M	9	33
Brunnemer, Jemima	95	38
Bunker, Mary E	320	35
Burnside, Alice P	26	36
Burtelt, Ellen	184	38
Blurock, Charles P ... part of	371	38
Butler, Taylor	62	35
Burns, Mary ... part of	92	25
Butler, Noble C	15	14
Bundy, John P ... part of	266	35

OWNERS' NAMES.	Lot No.	Section
Buehler, Annie	327	38
Burns, Harry G. and Elizabeth F	31	37
Budenz, Julia A	107	14
Buchanan, Anna .... part of	118	32
Burbridge, Alexander .... part of	49	37
Burton, John C	13 and 17	22
Buell, Chester H	72	15
Burton, Charles Henry	32	9
Buchanan, J. A .... part of	16	25
Buchanan, Oliver H .... part of	48	21
Bugbee, Francis M .... part of	8	15
Blue, Gerard	38	21
Butler, George	153	25
Burns, John B .... part of	30	9
Buscher, Mary E	189	32
Burns, Ella .... part of	212	32
Blue, Elizabeth and others	19	5
Burkhart, Louis C .... part of	92	20
Busking, Henry F	14	39
Burgess, Benjamin F	239	37
Bruce, Emanuel	223	37
Bruckman, John	274	38
Bruce, Augusta G	394	39
Bushong, Deniza .... part of	392	38
Blume, David L	343	37
Burgess, Anne J	123	25
Burton, Nellie M	442	37
Byrket, J. W	27	5
Bryan, Bennett	21	4
Byrd, James M	94	2
Blythe, William M	56	16
Byram, Norman S .... part of	42	14
Bly, John N .... part of	85	19
Bybee, Addison .... part of	15	23
Bryce, Peter F	93	27
Bryan, Zaritha	281	32
Byrn, William O	126	33
Byfield, Jessie M. A	336	32

OWNERS' NAMES.	Lot No.	Section
Byrket, Anna M. and others................	149	25
Byrket, Martin............................	88	37
Byers, Joseph M....................... part of	91	27
Bryson, John G........................ part of	26	14
Bryan, James W....................... part of	245	25
Bryant, Drusella...................... part of	7	39
Byfield, Vincent D........................	201	37
Carter, James W..........................	106, 108, 109	2
Carter, George...........................	134	2
Carter, John V...........................	107	2
Campbell, J. D...........................	31	4
Carter, George H.........................	60	5
Canby, Samuel....................... part of	112 and 113	4
Carpenter, Nathaniel......................	70 and 106	4
Chapman, Gen'l Geo. H...................	12	6
Craighead, D............................	8	1
Craig, Alexander.........................	139	4
Craig, W. R.............................	56	4
Chapman, David C........................	102	4
Craine, William N.................... part of	20	23
Carson, Mrs. Lydia A.....................	71	4
Craft, Mrs. A. G.........................	50	12
Carter, Robert...........................	120	4
Case, Elon E............................	58	2
Caldwell, H. W...................... part of	1	16
Charles, Mary....................... part of	63	16
Cathcart, Robert W.................. part of	46	12
Carter, William E........................	139	16
Clark, Maggie...........................	61	17
Cale, Howard...........................	3	12
Carey, Jason S...........................	70	14
Craig, R. A........................ part of	27	17
Chandler, Thomas E......................	17	7
Carter, Harlen...........................	88	20
Crane, George W.................... part of	64	15
Cain, Mrs. Eliza Ann.....................	27	20
Craig, Mrs. Mary E.................. part of	9	15
Clark, Rev'd I. N................... part of	33	21

OWNERS' NAMES.	Lot No.	Section
Catterson, Robert F............................ part of	25	13
Carven, Austin A.................................	101	25
Caylor, Magdalena.......................... part of	52	21
Campbell, Robert................................	114	25
Caylor, Jefferson................................	63	25
Clark, Daniel R..................................	154	31
Carter, Edward..................................	157	31
Clark, Stephen A............................ part of	137	27
Campbell, Mrs. Mary...........................	61	27
Catherwood, Mrs. Joseph.................. part of	14	23
Canan, John Thomas...........................	162	31
Chambers, James................................	27	31
Carter, Vinson...................................	145	27
Campbell, Sarah S...............................	236	31
Catterson, William T. and Elizabeth A .... part of	139	31
Campbell, Quintin...............................	175	31
Cantrill, Daniel M...............................	8	31
Carriger, John J.................................	297	31
Cady, David.................................. part of	67	19
Capito, Sarah J..................................	272	31
Clark, Charles A................................	262	31
Crane, William A...............................	22	32
Cain, Emily Jane................................	229	31
Callahan, John P................................	221	32
Clay, Hilary.................................. part of	28	8
Clarke, James E. and William H...............	292	31
Claypool, Solomon..............................	13	14
Chamberlain, J. H...............................	254	32
Craft, W. H.................................. part of	35	3
Cadwallader, John...............................	61	18
Carr, Mary A................................ part of	25	13
Clark, Charlott C................................	5	18
Carey, Elizabeth.................................	40	18
Carleton, Philip J. and George T .... part of	16	13
Caskey, James C............................ part of	315	32
Carter, Hester...................................	102	18
Carter, Catharine Ann and others..............	4	29
Claypool, Edward F.............................	7	29

OWNERS' NAMES.		Lot No.	Section
Chapman, John A	part of	134	33
Carter, Brice M		178	34
Caldwell, Andrew		166	32
Chantler, Mary		163	34
Cameron, Mrs. Mary E., heirs of		249	18
Caldwell, Jefferson		46	34
Cannon, William T		90	27
Catt, Milton		51	34
Crawford, Flora C		271	18
Chapman, Jennie		71	34
Carey, Simeon B		5	29
Chapin, Mary E		64	34
Craig, James	part of	340	32
Crawford, Thomas	part of	74	34
Caylor, Catherine		172	34
Case, Henry C	sub 4	1	17
Carroll, Christopher		87	34
Carey, Mary E. N	part of	15	29
Cramer, Charles H	sub 3	1	17
Carpenter, Rebecca A	part of	16	34
Carlisle, Mary J	subs 6 and 9	85	20
Charles, Benjamine	sub 2	71	20
Cahill, John S	sub 2	9	20
Campbell, Addie M	part of	383	32
Chase, William H		161	35
Campbell, Milton T		196	35
Clark, William H		200	35
Cahill, Thomas B		129	34
Caldwell, Charles C	part of	234	25
Clark, Joshua J	part of	103	35
Carter, John	part of	29	4
Clayton, Leonidas W		80	33
Craig, Luella M	part of	368	32
Cameron, John D. and Sarah E		72	35
Claffey, Frederick		216	35
Canby, Louisa H		1	9
Clark, Benjamin A		152	35
Case, William H		215	35

OWNERS' NAMES.

Name	Lot No.	Section
Craig, Joshua W .... part of	88	35
Clark, Sarah H .... sub 11	25	20
Cain, Michael	54	38
Chalmers, James H	69	36
Clapp, Jennie B	75	38
Clark, George M. D	13	38
Carlisle, Margaret Boyd	1	38
Crane, Julia Frances	114	38
Carll, Samuel P. and Mary	5	38
Clark, Alfred, Francis M. and William P	373 and 374	38
Craig, Richard B	33	37
Chapman, Amanda J	363	38
Castle, Maria L .... part of	372	38
Case, Martha A	360	38
Campbell, Walter	85	37
Claiborne, Leonard A	390	38
Campbell, Luther T. and Charles	358	38
Clay, Charlott A	12	37
Crawford, David S .... part of	75	36
Castor, Edwin A .... part of	35	5
Caffyn, Ellsworth	115	37
Crabb, John S. and John H	281	38
Caldwell, Elizabeth	33	39
Carothers, Missouri E .... part of	65	34
Clark, Alexander N. and Joseph H .... sub 6	64	13
Claybourne, Colin W	331	38
Crago, America C	309	35
Carey, Mary S .... part of	38	29
Clark, William F	43	39
Craig, Mary Henry .... part of	179	31
Carmichael, Margaret B .... part of	10	33
Craig, James F .... part of	368	32
Chapman, William J	159	39
Catterson, George N., executor	188	37
Clark, Perry F	66	4
Cranor, Andrew P	160	39
Catterson, Thomas L	123	39
Caldwell, James	117	39

OWNERS' NAMES.	Lot No.	Section
Chapman, Wilson and Hannah	227	37
Clark, Josephine E	137	39
Castenholz, Richard C	398	39
Craven, Dennis C	263	39
Campbell, William W	391	39
Camphausen, Louisa	338	37
Caffee, John H	24	32
Champe, Lida P	204	37
Chambers, Andrew J	352	37
Chapin, James W	273	38
Carter, Edward	195	39
Cravens, Junius E	174	4
Carmack, Harry W	353	37
Crandall, Joseph M	144	36
Caylor, Mary P part of	212	31
Chase, Rhoda J	39	9
Clayton, Henry and Hiram	264	37
Camphausen, Gottlieb	333	37
Chamberlain, William H	241	37
Carll, Samuel P	421	37
Carter, Gray W	244	37
Center, Capital and Germania Lodges, I. O. O. F.	51	7
Cleaveland, John B	33	12
Cherry, Elizabeth	3	5
Cleveland, Columbus, Cincinnati & Indianapolis R. R. Co.	104	25
Cheek, Edmond C	150	2
Cress, John B part of	331	31
Chestnutt, John	186	32
Cleaver, Jefferson	124	18
Cheely, George W	66	18
Clements, Thomas L	88	18
Cleary, John W part of	6	7
Clemmons, George W	72	34
Clements, Mrs. Ida B	287	18
Chester, Albert A	86	35
Clements, Leo	317	35
Clearwater, Martha	173	38
Cleaver, William T	236	37

OWNERS' NAMES.

Name	Lot No.	Section
Creemer, Daniel F.	321	39
Creed, Lavina E.	388	37
Cherry, Myrtle .... part of	87	20
Cressler, Clara	78	39
Clippinger, Mrs. Annie L.	14	12
Childers, Calvin F. .... part of	20	9
Criqui, Michael	30	21
Clines, Isaac H. .... part of	26	17
Clifford, Amos	7	27
Cline, Barney, Hiram and Marion	246	31
Christian, Mary	76	32
Crillman, David .... part of	119	33
Chipman, John W.	100	34
Chill, Charles F.	135	34
Chill, Thomas M.	134	34
Clippinger, Laura .... part of	197	35
Cline, William and Mahala .... part of	189	38
Childrens' Guardians', Board of	141	37
Chislett, Frederick W.	14	14
Chill, William F.	123	34
Chill, John W. F.	124	34
Crimans, William W.	205	37
Crimp, Mrs. W. G.	176	32
Chisman, James M. .... part of	393	39
Christofferson, Myrtle .... part of	124	39
Christy, Rachel C.	363	37
Chitwood, William M. .... part of	448	37
Coe, Isaac, estate of	67	1
Copeland, Joshua W.	12	2
Cook, Jane	17	2
Colestock, Ephraim	64	5
Cooper, J. J.	6	29
Cox, Leander	144	4
Cox, William	76	4
Connard, C. .... part of	33	2
Colgan, Henry G.	120	2
Comegys, Levi	146	2
Coley, Mrs. Louisa .... part of	17	1

OWNERS' NAMES.		Lot No.	Section
Coburn, Mrs. Mary A	part of	12	12
Cox, W. A		98	4
Collar, Mrs. Amanda		127	4
Cropsey, Mrs. Ann M		22	16
Colter, Richard S		44	16
Corliss, Corydon T	part of	65	3
Croft, Eliza, heirs of		197	16
Cook, Thomas V		179	16
Coffman, John S		150	16
Cox, Edward T	part of	65	3
Costelo, John J		32	3
Cox, Charles H		79	15
Connely, Robert	part of	11	13
Cooper, William H	part of	101	15
Coughlen, William		61	13
Council, Thomas W., John F. and Thomas J		179	4
Cornelius, Edward G	part of	42	14
Coffin, David W		7	4
Cole, B. W. and E. B		43	12
Coval, Willis	part of	16	9
Conklin, Mrs. Margaret		15	25
Conway, W. B	part of	12	25
Commingore, William H		61	21
Crozier, George		124	25
Coulan, Patrick		136	25
Coffin, Carrie E		90	25
Colden, John E		119	25
Condo, Elizabeth A		47	27
Cost, A. S		54 and 91	31
Cost, Charles A		90	31
Cost, George P		55	31
Coffin, William J		118	31
Cook, Joseph		235	31
Cromlich, Mary E		12	31
Coyner, Susan M		186	27
Coffman, Miss Ella		302	31
Coffin, Mary B		224	32
Conner, John B	part of	53	22

CROWN HILL CEMETERY.

OWNERS' NAMES.		Lot No.	Section
Colebrook, Frederick J		8 and 9	32
Coe, Orris K	part of	21	23
Covert, William T		200	32
Cornelius, P. S	part of	324	31
Conde, H. T		48	22
Collins, William F		219	31
Coleman, Mrs. Mary E		302	32
Cross, Polly	part of	149	27
Conaroe, Asa B		328	32
Collier, William S		75	20
Cochran, Thomas F	part of	291	32
Cook, Frank G	part of	280	32
Collier, Thomas		196 and 198	18
Coulter, James W		53	18
Colter, Margaret		74 and 84	18
Cloud, Robert T. S		21	25
Crosby, John S	part of	105	27
Cook, Noah	part of	109	27
Cotten, Perry W		133 and 144	18
Conklin, Kate		251 and 265	18
Coffin, Arthur and Eunice A		379	32
Cochrane, Samuel W		30	34
Comstock, Horace A		82	34
Crowley, Henrietta		183	34
Cornelius, Cassius		332	32
Cookerly, John M		359	32
Coburn, John and Henry	part of	136	27
Cook, Henry		166	34
Cosler, Mary E	part of	116	33
Cobb, Julia B	part of	4	5
Condell, Mrs. Mary J. and Jennie R		146	34
Collins, Major	part of	257	25
Cook, John and Rosina		376	32
Crowe, George W		147	33
Campagne, Virginia	sub 1	92	20
Cottman, John A	sub 2	72	20
Cooper, Hamilton	part of	105	33
Crowder, Burrel	sub 1	81	17

OWNERS' NAMES.	Lot No.	Section
Cox, Nellie.	162	35
Cordes, Herman.	334	31
Coffin, Barnabas...........................part of	69	4
Closser, Louise M........................part of	89	14
Compton, Samuel M. and Mary E.	6	33
Courtney, Sarah.	163	35
Coen, Mary.	95	35
Cron, Adam.	207	35
Cook, John W.	3	35
Cox, John A. M. and Kate A.	257	35
Coleman, John G.........................part of	30	38
Coulter, Charles W......................part of	36	36
Cross, Frank P.	58	38
Copeland, James M.	33	38
Cooney, Rebecca E......................part of	179	27
Copelin, Samuel.	103	37
Crowe, Lewis S.	84	38
Cox, Millard F.	318	35
Corbaley, William H.	241	35
Cotton, Jennie...........................part of	76	38
Coleman, Benjamin F....................part of	30	38
Conduitt, Alexander B.	68	29
Coffin, Mollie...........................part of	5	20
Coffman, Martha E......................part of	86	20
Colter, Andrew J.......................part of	5	20
Comstock, James M.	362	38
Conaway, Edward.........................part of	167	38
Coffin, Carrie E.	57	37
Cowles, Edward W.	351	38
Cox, Edward.	319	38
Cook, Eliza M............................part of	109	27
Cross, John William.....................part of	294	35
Combs, Dr. George W....................part of	97	14
Connor, William S.	65	37
Cox, Mrs. Addie.	283	38
Cotton, Isaac M.	357	38
Coffin, Albert W........................part of	7	4
Collins, James L.	192	37

CROWN HILL CEMETERY.

OWNERS' NAMES.		Lot No.	Section
Crosley, Henry	part of	52	25
Cross, Mary A	sub 3	71	20
Coyle, Josephine	part of	169	37
Coffin, Abraham		304	38
Cowan, Harriet, heirs of		230	39
Conarroe, Mattie J	part of	142	39
Coleman, Milton H		12	33
Coble, Mary Ann		204	39
Conner, Charles O		172	39
Coval, Lena		144	39
Cobb, Samuel H		102	39
Cones, Joseph T	part of	196	36
Coval, Charles H		221	39
Connor, Robert		166	39
Crowley, Daniel F		192	39
Cooper, Elijah and Ellsworth		228	37
Cox, Charles E	part of	87	39
Cooley, Samuel M	part of	87	39
Cosby, Hiram		187	39
Converse, Elenor M	part of	224	37
Crossman, Elizabeth A		326	37
Cochran, William M		221	36
Condrey, Edgar		346	37
Connett, M. F	part of	17	35
Cones, Mrs. Natalie M	part of	64	3
Conover, George W		311	31
Coffin, Cannon O		325	39
Coleman, Benjamin F	part of	323	37
Cones, Nancey G		184	36
Corey, Mattie L	part of	130	39
Coffin, Charles E	part of	26	14
Cook, Hugo	part of	182	16
Cooper, Martha Jane		47	34
Comely, Emily J		84	34
Cook, David P		341	37
Cookus, Eveline		428	37
Cloud, Mrs. C. T	part of	392	37
Coburn, Lydia		514	39

A FOREST PARK.

OWNERS' NAMES.		Lot No.	Section
Coffy, Adelbert B	part of	362	39
Cotton, Ellen M		520	39
Churchman, F. M		31	6
Culbertson, William	part of	57	2
Culley, D. V	part of	7	12
Cummings, Thomas		176	16
Curtis, C. T	part of	17	19
Curlee, W. A		14	19
Cummins, Mrs. Frances A	part of	57	15
Currie, Mary P	part of	24 and 25	21
Crull, David		10	27
Cunningham, Yorick F		88	32
Cunningham, Mrs. Martha		47	32
Curtis, Mary		180	32
Church, Joseph H		148	32
Culloden, Frederick	part of	38	33
Cushing, Charles		53	33
Cullum, Eberle		158	33
Cunningham, Henry S	part of	2 and 3	33
Curson, William J		165	35
Cruse, James S	part of	150	27
Cukow, George	part of	87 and 88	35
Cunningham, Mrs. Tracy	part of	27	38
Curzon, Joseph	part of	61	14
Cutter, Harry Page		344	35
Cummins, Frances A	part of	22	21
Curtis, Lyman W	part of	127	27
Culmann, Wilhelmina	part of	29	39
Curson, John F		211	39
Culbertson, Walter L		156	37
Churchill, Leroy S	part of	150	36
Cunningham, Catharine		271	37
Currens, Hamilton		280	37
Cullen, Minnie	part of	31	21
Cummings, Mrs. Anna		498	39
Crusius, Sarah V		499	39
Davidson, D. N. and P. A		13	1
Danforth, Albert J		37	1

OWNERS' NAMES.	Lot No.	Section
Davis, William M....................................	57	4
Dawson, Henry......................................	79	4
Davis, Mrs. Sarah C.................... part of	55	3
Davis, John L.......................................	15	4
Davis, Charles B....................................	48	2
Dain, Robert C.....................................	58	16
Darnell, Calvin F...................... part of	183	16
Davis, Joseph W....................................	59	15
Darrow, Benjamin C.................................	16	15
Davis, Joseph and Mary................ part of	46	19
Daugherty, J. F....................................	83	19
Darfel, Mary.......................................	68	21
Darnell, Z...	40	25
Davis, Mary E......................................	43	25
Davis, Wesley and Nathan...........................	141	25
Daumont, Charity J.................... part of	134	27
Dawson, John W....................................	194	27
Davidson, John........................ part of	90	2
Davis, Annie.......................................	102	31
Darnell, William and J. W..........................	177	31
Davis, Marietta E..................................	1	29
Daubenspeck, Greenbury.............................	133	31
Darnell, Calvin F..................... part of	14	23
Dailey, Hezekiah...................................	240	32
Dasher, Lillie M. and Grace L......... part of	284	32
Davis, Charles.....................................	100	32
Davenport, Wm. H...................... part of	239	25
Dawson, Jackson....................... part of	182	27
Davis, James C. and William E......................	228	18
Daniels, Mrs. Mary M..............................	184	27
Darling, Walter....................................	118	18
Davis, Lambert D...................................	111	34
Davis, Benjamin....................................	160	34
Darling, Delamy M.................... part of	96	34
David, George F...................... part of	239	25
Dawson, Byron........................ part of	228	25
Danke, Albert......................................	310	18
Day, Martha M....................... sub 4	92	20

OWNERS' NAMES.	Lot No.	Section
Daniels, Mary B .... part of	155	27
Davis, Alma B.......................	49	16
Dahl, Catherine.....................	148	35
Davis, Willard and Zillah	304	35
Davis, Robert.......................	57	35
Danforth, Ovias J...................	162	33
Danz, Catherine Elizabeth	128	35
David, Ettie........................	193	35
David, William C .... part of	239	25
Davis, William E .... part of	81	17
Dark, Charles E. and Margaret R.......	67	29
Danner, James H...................	259	35
Davis, Eliza....................... part of	16	38
Davidson, Christopher C..............	57	38
Davis, Jennie D.....................	198	35
Daly, Mary H .... part of	72	38
Davison, Nora......................	117	38
Darrow, Margaret J .... part of	8	38
David, Nettie..................... part of	77	37
Daniels, Wm. E .... part of	25	38
David, Joseph F .... part of	109	35
Davis, Eliza........................	341	38
Daubenspeck, Nelson (Trustee)	296	35
Davis, Mark S......................	196	36
Davidson Belle .... part of	206	39
Davis, John R .... part of	286	39
Drapier, William H., Jr	70	18
Davis, Waldo T.....................	159	37
Davis, Mary........................	494	39
Davidson, Jane .... part of	22	19
Dallas, Isabella.....................	523	39
Daglish, John	6 and 7	32
Daly, George W....................	309	37
Davenport, John F..................	466	39
Davis, Mary H.....................	286	37
Deaver, G. W.................... part of	80	5
Drew, S. W .... part of	19	3
Drew, J. H .... part of	19	3

OWNERS' NAMES.		Lot No.	Section
Decher, Conrad	part of	81	3
De Pew, Miletred	part of	112 and 113	4
Denny, Mrs. Elizabeth and Sons		8 and 9	4
Delzell, Samuel	part of	3	13
Deitzel, Mrs. Kate		96	4
Deaf and Dumb, Institute For		28, 29 and 48	7
Delzell, Hugh		72	5
Despa, Ernest		32	16
Denny, John E		171	16
Dearinger, Simon	part of	81	15
Dennerline, John		32	17
Delzell, Mary A		62	13
DeMott, William S	part of	91	16
Deller, Mrs. Kate	part of	23	20
Dell, William		4	4
Dreher, Matthias		55	19
De Haven, Edward C		25	27
De Haven, Anna E		33	27
Decker, J. E., J. H. and H. E.		203	25
Dewar, Duncan		67	32
Dean, John W. and Grace A		183	27
Dean, Joseph C		211	32
Devine, William		194	18
Deam, Mrs. Susan	part of	148	16
Dennis, Joseph H	part of	36	34
Dehne, Charles		14	34
Denny, Robert		193	34
Dennis, Peter		372	32
Dearinger, David		154	33
Desgardins, Adelheid	sub 7	25	20
Devore, Gus	sub 5	71	20
Denny, Hariet J	sub 4	82	17
De Poy, William B. and Mary E	part of	2	17
Denk, Andrew		181	35
Decker, Mary		231	35
De Hart, Juriah L		28	38
Degner, William		67	38
Denny, Samuel	part of	2	3

OWNERS' NAMES.	Lot No.	Section
Decker, Justus and Eliza	326	38
Decker, John	186	16
Dewald, Matthias	8	17
Dehne, William	95	36
Deschler, Nettie .... part of	155	39
De Hart, Pauline .... part of	27	38
Despo, Isidore .... part of	361	37
Delp, Otto	379	39
Dean, Benjamin F	277	39
De Vay, Mrs. Agnes V	60	14
Delzell, Samuel A	281	37
Dickey, James B	56	2
Dickson, Myron	48	12
Dietz, Fred	59	2
Dillman, M. R.	192	16
Dippell, Mary A	8	16
Dippell, Catherine	166	16
Dille, Sarah L	39	19
Dixon, James W .... part of	26	17
Dickson, Thomas M	107	15
Dickert, Jacob	132	25
Dickman, Francis	44	27
Dietz, Frances	36	27
Dixon, Minerva L	199	31
Dietz, Peter	190	25
Dickerson, William M	17	32
Dittemore, John W .... part of	331	31
Dietrichs, Emilie .... part of	338	32
Dickinson, Edward .... part of	110	27
Dillon, Alexander A	93	18
Dillingham, Albert .... part of	89	27
Dillon, Levi	278	18
Dickson, Mrs. James B .... part of	56	14
Dickson, Mary A	22	14
Dickson, Elizabeth G .... part of	92	27
Dickenson, Alice E. and Jane E	66	35
Drinkwater, Edward H	289	35
Dickerson, Landon F	119	38

OWNERS' NAMES.   Lot No.   Section

Name		Lot No.	Section
Dickert, Norbert A	...	51	36
Dillert, George W		135	38
Dickey, George C	part of	175	38
Dippel, John		348	38
Dickson, Francis	part of	183	18
Driesbaugh, Catherine		356	38
Dittman, John H. and Frederick		66	37
Dierks, Gert	part of	311	38
Dilley, John H	part of	323	37
Dimock, Daniel J		446	39
Dill, Elizabeth		179	37
Doughty, J. G		51	1
Donnan, Barbary		67	5
Donough, D. B		10	2
Douglas, James G., Samuel M. and Ellen B		1	14
Dorbecker, Louisa	part of	87	16
Downie, Mellisa E		69	2
Downey, Samuel R		6	9
Downas, William J	part of	10	9
Douglas, Andrew		31	25
Dollman, Charles		55	21
Dohn, Philip		117	25
Donaldson, Amanda		24	27
Dollarhide, Sarah		121	31
Donalt, Elizabeth		184	31
Doerr, George	part of	328	31
Dobson, Henry		325	32
Dorsey, Mrs. Effie		82	18
Downing, Michael A		9	29
Dougherty, Lafayette Richard		151	34
Downey, William B	part of	196	34
Doeppus, Charles	sub 2	58	20
Douglas, Mrs. Olive G	sub 9	92	20
Dougherty, Roxanna C	part of	35	35
Downie, Samuel C	part of	36	35
Dory, Joseph	part of	34	38
Dockweiler, Charles		10	36
Donivan, Ella	part of	340	32

CROWN HILL CEMETERY.

OWNERS' NAMES.	Lot No.	Section
Doene, Wilhelmina	229	18
Downing, Frank	333	38
Dobbs, Scipio	27	37
Douthitt, Flora A	93	2
Dockweiler, John	28	39
Dorsey, R. S .... part of	14	3
Dorbecker, Jacob H	16	16
Donovan, James R	157	39
Doran, Charles F	367	37
Doershell, Annie .... part of	301	38
Downie, William M	285	39
Downey, Helena M .... part of	301	39
Doolittle, Charles A	351	37
Downey, George .... part of	186	39
Dorsett, Missouri A .... part of	399	39
Dockweiler, Henry G .... part of	44	13
Donovan, Clara	79	39
Duzan, Dr. William N	21	1
Dunlap, J. S	7	2
Duncan, R. B	9 and 10	3
Duzan, George W .... part of	7	6
Dunbar, Mrs. Sarah	22	2
Dumont, Gen'l E	118	2
Dunn, John C	45	5
Durbin, David S	18	1
Dunning, Robert P .... part of	40	14
Dunn, Mrs. Maggie E	6	27
Dunlap, John M. and Mrs. Diautha	156	27
Duvall, Sophronia A. and Sarah D	195	25
Dury, John .... part of	4	15
Dunn, Jacob T. and Harriet L	371	32
Du Graurut, Elizabeth	157, 158, 179	18
Dunn, Edward	4	35
Dunn, George E	157	35
Duncan, Carrie J .... part of	87	20
Duncan, John A	141	38
Durve, William	133	38
Dunning, Samuel M .... part of	194	39

OWNERS' NAMES.	Lot No.	Section
Duncan, Robert	167	37
Duncan, Alexander W	316	37
Dunmeyer, Christian	408	39
Dryer, James W part of	245	25
Dye, Charity part of	20	23
Dryer, Charles A part of	192	27
Dye, Mary A part of	79	14
Dye, William W part of	91	27
Evans, Thomas P	61	2
Evans, Robert	15	5
Evans, Henry W	85	16
Evans, John D., Heirs of	19	14
Evans, Mrs. Maria J	12 and 13	15
Evans, Thomas	7	19
Evans, Wm. R., George T. and Joseph R.	63	13
Eagle, J. H.	156	25
Ewan, Albert O	89	31
Egan, Edward C part of	6	3
Eaton, Laura E part of	243	25
Egan, Thomas P	187	27
Earley, William A part of	139	32
Edwards, John	187	18
Eaglesfield, William	52	22
Earls, Thomas D	136	33
Earls, Silas J	89	18
Evans, Mary A	119	18
Edwards, Jacob B	66	34
Earnshaw, Joseph	9	34
Esamann, Mary K part of	182	16
Essmann, Gertrude part of	341	31
Evans, Page Cheek part of	155	27
Elam, John B	344	32
Evans, Joseph part of	29	4
Edwards, Alexander	138	35
Erhart, Barbara part of	303	35
Evans, Clarissa Ann part of	120	38
Eaglin, George R	110	38
Ewald, Henry	318	38

OWNERS' NAMES.	Lot No.	Section
Evans, William R.	333	35
Eaton, Benjamin A.	23	12
Egan, Michael.	172	18
Eades, James M.	414	37
Earl, John	445	39
East, Thomas J........part of	354	39
Elff, Frank	233	32
Evans, Samuel J.	426	37
Elder, William G.	78	4
Egerton, Charles	74	2
Estler, Floyed.	33	16
Erdlemeyer, Franz	35	12
Eberhardt, George........part of	80	16
Emrich, Henry........part of	103	16
Ernst, Frederick.	68	16
Eberts, John.	46	21
Eden, Charlton........part of	47	3
Elbert, Caroline.	7	20
Engle, George B., Sr.	14	21
Emmett, Edith A.	54	14
Elder, John R.	35	23
Engelke, Frederick.	54	25
Emerson, Roswell B.	84	21
Ebner, John	288	31
Ehrensperger, Frank	205	25
Emmelmann, Henry	71 and 87	18
Eggert, William	37	18
Engle, Mary Ann	202	18
Egelus, Frederick........part of	118	33
Elbreg, Mrs. George.	283	18
Emley, Samuel C.	32	34
Eberhardt, Dora	150	34
Eberhardt, John.	19	34
Ebert, John.	34	33
Ellenwood, Emma........part of	64	3
Empey, George W........part of	350	32
Eberhardt, Emma	14	35
Everts, Orpheus.	14	36

CROWN HILL CEMETERY.

OWNERS' NAMES.		Lot No.	Section
Edenharter, George F. and Franklin T	part of	82	33
Ernestinoff, Alexander	part of	190	38
Edgeworth, Mrs. Lula		98	37
Eden, Charles M		377	38
Eden, Henry		367	38
Engelking, William		179	36
Eckel, George F		354	38
Eggert, Bertha H	part of	343	38
Ellenberger, John		230	36
Eggert, Ferdinand	part of	25	39
Espey, Henry		45	33
Emerich, Frank P	part of	72	17
Egger, Rebecca	part of	116	37
Eshleman, Ella V	part of	73	19
Egelhoff, Henry	part of	340	39
Elder, Catherine E		242	39
Eberhardt, John G., Sr. and John G., Jr		269	39
Elder, Eli A		331	39
Everett, David T		427	37
Elliott, Pernetta	part of	3	3
Ervin, Edmond P		44	17
Ewick, Johnson H		52	15
Elliott, William S		18	17
English, William H		72	1
English, J. M		145	25
Elliott, Jonathan		19	23
Elliott, Calvin A	part of	18	23
Ellison, Fred		111	31
Einatz, Olive G		79	27
Elliott, Joseph T	part of	50	3
Elvin, Gardner William	part of	42	20
Eitel, Henry	part of	151	27
Ehrich, William		58	32
Elliott, John M		101 and 102	32
Elliott, Ashley J		114	32
Ellis, Mary A	part of	139	32
Etris, Mary	part of	314	31
Emswiler, Lizzie	part of	31	13

OWNERS' NAMES.	Lot No.	Section
Eldridge, Jacob	96	34
Elliott, James Perry	77	18
Elliott, Sarah P. ... part of	196	34
Emrich, John H. ... part of	101	33
Eldrigde, William K.	351	35
Ellis, Thomas L.	55	35
Ellinger, Reuben	210	35
Emrich, Christina ... part of	359 and 360	35
Emrich, William F. ... part of	359	35
Elliott, William G.	62	36
Elvin, Robert J. ... part of	252	25
English, Henry	124	38
Eifert, Catherine	96	36
Emrich, Jacob A. ... part of	360	35
Ellis, Robert G.	105	39
Elliott, Charlotte H.	138	39
Elliott, Louisa C.	372	39
Ellis, Sallie A.	282	32
Ennis, Charles W. and Mabel	47	13
Elliott, John L.	577	39
Essigke, Richard	273	39
Eldridge, Milton ... part of	362	37
Eilering, Levi and Benjamin	477	39
Ehrisman, Mrs. Mary	517	39
Eilhard, Frederick C. ... part of	311	39
Emmons, John B.	48	16
Echols, H. H. ... part of	36	15
Eoff, Margaret Louisa	190	31
Echols, Alice	195	18
Emory, Mrs. Francis	92	18
Enos, Trovello H. K.	367	35
Ehrgott, Emil ... part of	7	35
Escott, Mary Elizabeth	73	37
Edmondson, George F.	59	37
Echols, John T. ... part of	247	39
Elstrod, Henry	479	39
Edmunds, William	58	1
Ensey, John	169	35

OWNERS' NAMES.	Lot No.	Section
Eurich, Mary............................part of	4	21
Eddy, Morris R..........................part of	2	5
Ely, John C. F..............................	356	37
Ely, Lillie..............................part of	456	39
Emry, Joseph H. and James H................	244	31
Endly, Thomas E. and John A................	15	35
Eddy, Horace J. and Eugenia S.........part of	2	5
Fahnestock, Mrs. Elizabeth..................	10	4
Franzman, Adam............................	25	4
Falkner, J. B..............................	13	5
Frank, Frances I......................part of	159	2
Frankem, Jonathen..........................	56	3
Fatout, M. K..............................	8	8
Frazee, William D..........................	14	16
Flack, Joseph F.......................part of	8	3
Fahrbach, Philip...........................	21	15
Farquhar, Mrs. Fanny M................part of	29	12
Fauckner, Joseph H.........................	12	20
Frank, Henry..........................part of	66 and 73	15
Fawcett, A. H..............................	8	9
Flanders, John B...........................	72	21
Fahnley, Fred.........................part of	60	13
Francis, T. S..............................	35	25
Francis, J. T..........................part of	7	15
Flack, Joseph.........................part of	32	23
Failey, J. W...............................	122	25
Fay, Jean..................................	50	27
Farmer, Jerome B......................part of	144	27
Frazier, Mary K............................	164	31
Frauer, Rudolph............................	36	5
Faulkinburg, W. S.....................part of	231 and 232	31
Frauer, Albert G...........................	326	31
Frazee, Mrs. Samuel E.................part of	24	23
Fahrion, Christian.........................	62	31
Frankenstein, Kate.........................	156	18
Faries, T. C...............................	157	27
Farnham, Mrs. Jerusha.................part of	179	31
Fairfield, Mrs. Florinda...................	27	33

OWNERS' NAMES.	Lot No.	Section
Farley, William..	339	35
Fahrbach, Kate..	130	37
Franz, Margaret..................... part of	22	19
Francis, Isabella..................... part of	194	38
Franklin, Columbus A and Rose........... part of	68	19
Fatout, Hervey B. and Daniel H........... part of	8	6
Flack, John S..................... part of	8	3
Flanner, Orpha A..	157	16
Faucher, John..	290	38
Franklin, William..	180	37
Frantz, Mary Katherine............. part of	204	38
Faucett, James E. and Charles E................	122	39
Farger, Elizabeth..................... part of	27	9
Farra, Annette L..	309	39
Faust, Michael..................... part of	314	32
Fahrbach, Emma..................... part of	117	16
Farrabee, Emma..	332	39
Failey, James F..	102	14
Fahrion, John George....................................	229	37
Flathers, Jennie..	240	37
Fletcher, Gertrude N....................................	5	6
Fletcher, Stoughton A., Jr............................	13 and 14	7
Fletcher, Ingram..	11	7
Fletcher, Stoughton A., Sr............................	12	7
Fletcher, Elijah T..	10	7
Fletcher, Calvin, Sr....................................	8 and 9	7
Fleming, Mrs. Mary....................................	34	2
French, C. G..................... part of	36	7
Ferguson, J. C..................... part of	13, 14, 16, 17, 18	8
Ferguson, John A..	152	2
Frenzel, John P..	82	2
Ferguson, Edward H....................................	154	2
Fletcher, S. K..	15	7
Fletcher, A. E..	63	7
Freeman, Sarah P..	45 and 53	4
Ferre, Mrs. Mary..	66	3
Featherston, William E............. part of	2	4
Feiner, Julius..	9	17

OWNERS' NAMES.	Lot No.	Section
Frech, Henry	82	16
Fletcher, Thomas A	80	20
Fletcher, Mary F......... part of	13	9
Fletcher, W. M.......... part of	13	9
Freihling, M.	4	9
Ferguson, Robert H	127	25
Fetrow, Joseph	36	25
Ferry, Mrs. Jane	126	4
Ferger, Charles	86	25
Ferling, Eliza M. C.	112	25
Fehr, Christ	46	27
Fette, George	82	19
Fletcher, Allen M.	68 and 69	7
Fletcher, Stoughton J.	65 and 66	7
Ferree, Shadrach L.	194	32
Fleming, John S.......... part of	245	31
Fette, Mrs. A. M........ part of	42	7
Freeman, Anna M......... part of	248	32
Ferry, Mrs. Anna E....... part of	69	27
Ferguson, Ann V.	244	18
Fertig, Francis	42	33
Freeman, Mary A., James A., Emma L. B. and J. M.	98	27
Feller, Mrs. Maggie and John	166 and 171	18
Fee, Lorenzo	205	34
Frederick, Caroline........ part of	382	32
Fenton, John and J. H.	331	32
Ferry, Mrs. Ida	286	18
Frese, Magdalena	153	34
French, George W......... part of	257	25
Fletcher, Gertrude M...... part of	15	29
Feldkamp, Reinhard W.	240	35
Fenneman, Anna C	20	35
Ferguson, Isaac	58	35
Fleming, Caroline	73	35
Ferguson, James A. and David S	265	35
Fleming, Nora	271	35
Fellows, Lewis L.	8	33
Freiburg, John	49	38

PART OF SECTION TWENTY-THREE.

OWNERS' NAMES.   Lot No.   Section

Ferrell, Mary L..	79	38
Fletcher, James L................ part of	3	15
Frederichs, Caroline............. part of	118	38
Fleckhammer, Charles........... part of	4	20
Ferguson, William Carl.......... part of	171	38
Free, John W....................	191	38
Ferguson, Henry C...............	68	37
Fletcher, Henry F............... part of	127	27
Feely, Daniel................... part of	239	36
Fertig, Frank...................	11	36
Feuchter, Chris.................	299	38
Feller, Mattie.................. part of	3	17
Ferguson, C. A.................. part of	6	6
Fenneman, Henry W...............	54	1
Freeman, Milton E...............	37	39
Featherston, Rhea............... part of	2	4
Fleck, John..................... part of	210	37
Fleming, Sophia.................	220	37
Fessler, Levi H.................	216	37
Fletcher, Anna E................ part of	186	18
Fiscus, Andrew J................	163	4
Frizzell, Bushrod...............	23	4
Frizzell, Allen.................	167	4
Fishback, Mrs. Sarah J..........	95	2
Fish, John L....................	62	1
Finney, Jasper..................	36	2
Finn, Mrs. Elizabeth............	11	4
Fish, William S.................	61	1
Frink, Erastus O................	28	15
Fishback, John..................	84	31
Fike, John W.................... part of	201	25
Fiedler, Christian G............	230	32
Fink, Mrs. Mary and Frederick R.. part of	202	25
Fiscus, Elizabeth............... part of	212	32
Friedgen, C..................... part of	13	3
Frick, Philip J.................	104	32
Fitch, W. H.................... part of	6	7
Fritsche, Christian C........... part of	227	31

OWNERS' NAMES.		Lot No.	Section
Fritsche, Reinhold C.	part of	227	31
Fisher, Nancy	part of	319	31
Fisher, Henry		250	18
Fisher, Robert D.		162	34
Friedgen, Wilhelmina		176	18
Friedley, Harmon H	part of	238	25
Fitzgerald, Joseph		300	18
Frick, John	part of	109	33
Fisher, Frank and Elizabeth.	part of	29	15
Firmin, Florence	sub 3	81	17
Finch, Theodore J		60	35
Findling, Abraham		187	35
Fike, Laura J	part of	24	9
Flick, William B	part of	159	32
Fisher, Joseph L		51	39
Fish, Elizabeth	part of	353	38
Fisk, Henry Clay		225	36
Fricker, George C	part of	202	39
Fishback, William P	part of	77	14
Fish, Lewis C.		149	39
Fickle, Manington		302	38
Field, John W		183	39
Field, Martin H		250	25
Finley, Theresa		264	39
Finitzer, John		329	39
Fike, Jacob and Laura J		23	9
Fisher, Otto		443	39
Foote, Maria W		71	2
Foster, Riley		28	2
Foos, Thomas J		40	1
Foley, Charles		114	2
Foley, Susannah C		31	12
Fortner, Calvin		115	16
Foster, Edgar J		73	17
Fogerty, Charles J		61	20
Forbes, Joseph R. and Lettie A	part of	50	14
Fort, John W		29	27
Foudray, John E	part of	137	27

CROWN HILL CEMETERY.

OWNERS' NAMES.		Lot No.	Section
Fortner, Josephine and Fannie	part of	38	12
Fortner, Sanford	part of	38	12
Foster, R. S	part of	11	15
Foust, Charles J	part of	11	15
Foster, Chapin C	part of	195	27
Froi De Vaux, Aug. A		129	32
Foss, Justin O		296	32
Foudray, Edgar E		105 and 106	32
Foulds, Thomas I		103	32
Ford, Eliza T		67	18
Foster, Roger M		242	18
Fortney, Charles		237	18
Fosdyke, Arthur G	part of	24	34
Foster, Annie E		255	18
Foster, Sarah	part of	16	35
Forsinger, George Clarence		10	35
Foland, Milton	part of	119	35
Foltz, Howard M	part of	8	13
Foster, Martha J		360	32
Flowers, Daisy D		97	37
Foreman, Mary M		55	37
Foster, Elizabeth Sewell	part of	119	34
Foy, Owen		276	38
Flowers, Naomi		138	37
Foster, Benjamin F	part of	223	32
Froschauer, Charles P. and Rosa		4	39
Folsom, David K., Heirs of		258	36
Fox, Rany		25	36
Foster, Barbara	part of	341	39
Forbes, Corydon A		376	39
Forshee, George W., Sr., and George W., Jr		391	37
Forsyth, William and Elijah J., Jr		298	39
Fugate, James F		42	5
Fulton, William H. and Isabella		91	15
Funkhouser, David, Heirs of	part of	12	11
Fulmer, C. H		102	25
Furchkenicht, Ernst		42	21
Fulton, Frank P		43	27

OWNERS' NAMES.	Lot No.	Section
Fulton, Robert	180	31
Funk, Amer J	18	32
Furgason, James M .... part of	239	25
Furgason, William C	18	34
Furnas, John	356	32
Furnas, Robert W .... part of	60	36
Furgason, Mellison	193	37
Fullgraff, Elizabeth and Otto	69	39
Fulmer, Leander A	205	36
Furgason, Albert L	251	38
Fulton, Sarah C	193	32
Fry, Robert L	10	19
Frybarger, John and Sarah M	349	37
Gaston, Dr. John M	27	3
Gardner, Conrad	29	3
Graham, George	35	4
Gates, John J	55	2
Galloway, Mrs. Kizzie W	78	2
Graydon, Mrs. Jane C	15	3
Gallahue, Phœnix M	96	2
Graves, Lewis W .... part of	2	12
Gates, Alfred B .... part of	5	3
Graham Samuel J	108	14
Glazier, Lydia	31	15
Glazier, Mrs. Fannie	30	15
Graham, David A	31	20
Gabert, Mary .... part of	109	16
Gaeth, Fred .... part of	63	21
Glazier, Francis H .... part of	7	15
Gaston, Mrs. H. R	46	14
Gaston, Edward, Jr., and William	40	21
Garver, M	160	25
Gayle, W. G	120	25
Glasscock, William .... part of	171	25
Gass, George H	88	27
Gray, Mrs. Helen	12	22
Gauss, Matilda	85	27
Garner, Horatio S	218	25

OWNERS' NAMES.		Lot No.	Section
Gabel, Conrad	part of	179 and 180	25
Grasbling, N.		29	31
Gardner, W. H		135	31
Grandstaff, Ada and Emma	part of	18	25
Gaul, Frederick W		44	32
Gale, C. C.	part of	57	14
Grant, Emma L.		15	32
Gardner, Wendel		231	32
Graham, Mrs. M. E	part of	188	32
Graeber, Emerson L		68	32
Gahm, Magdalena		213	32
Gardner, C. J.		216	31
Garver, John J	part of	162	27
Gable, Lewis A	part of	162	27
Grafenstein, Frederick	part of	161	27
Gaunt, Belle E.	part of	2	17
Graham, Robert D. and Nancy A	part of	170	32
Gray, Mrs. Susannah	part of	254	25
Gakstatter, Philip		240	18
Gardner, William H		140	34
Galvin, John F.		267	18
Grant, William F		152	34
Ganerdinger, Jacob J	part of	44	7
Gay, Mary		129	35
Gray, Susannah	part of	72	3
Galbraith, Jane		184	34
Graeter, Elizabeth		205	35
Glaescher, Frederick	part of	78	35
Gardner, Mary A		267	35
Gardner, Thomas W		18	38
Gass, Emma	part of	45	15
Gray, William Henry		297	35
Graham, Frank W. and Fannie S		325	38
Graber, Frederick		320	38
Gauld, John D. and Alexander B		139 and 140	37
Gray, Mahala	part of	23	17
Grassow, Catherine D	part of	35	21
Glass, Christopher C	part of	204	34

OWNERS' NAMES.	Lot No.	Section
Grassow, Caroline	63	18
Gang, Joseph	190	39
Gambold, Levi S	182	39
Gramling, John C	319	39
Gary, Chas. J	246	39
Grace, Harry .... part of	173	16
Gray, Samuel F .... part of	135	36
Graham, William M	413	37
Gardner, Fred C	343	32
Gardner, Joseph	177	32
Garrish, Nathaniel W	311	37
Gausepohl, J. Fred .... part of	327	39
Gambold, Thomas E .... part of	356	39
Galt, Harry S	291	37
Gauding, Elizabeth .... part of	272	39
Granger, Martha J .... part of	202	39
Grady, Mrs. Lulu F	329	37
Gakstatter, Charles	21	38
Gray, Mary Jane	344	37
Gardner, John	304	37
Gladden, Alfred H	143	36
Geisel, H .... part of	81	3
Greenleaf, Edward .... part of	41	5
Greenleaf, Clements A	44	5
Gresh, John	61	16
Geis, John	47	16
Grein, John	69	16
Gessert, Fred	7	17
Gresh, Levi	89	15
Geiger, George W	11	9
Geisel, Henry E .... part of	13	21
Gerdts, John	24	4
Geizendanner, William	163	31
Green, John C., Robert L. and Lucian H	125	25
Gelzenleuchter, John ...... part of	300	31
Gregg, Aaron S	127	32
Greenrod, Timothy .... part of	223	31
Geisel, Christian	27	18

OWNERS' NAMES.	Lot No.	Section
Gerardy, Nicholas............ part of	328	31
Greene, James .... part of	233	25
Gregg, Sarah .... part of	4	29
Green, Herbert W............. part of	38	33
Green, Richard	52	33
Geisendorf, Christian E....... part of	191	27
Geisendorf, Lydia T..........	115	33
Geisler, John.................	255	32
Greilich, John .... part of	128	33
Greene, Charles P........... part of	45	16
Gehring, Lena............... part of	105	33
Greenfield, Jane............. part of	92	27
Greiner, Margaret...........	48	38
Gregg, Elizabeth............	131	38
Green, Henry...............	117 and 118	4
Gerhart, Mrs. Ormsby M.....	378	38
Geizendanner, John G....... part of	253	31
Green, Martha J............ part of	372	38
Greenlee, James S.......... part of	388	38
Gerard, Elizabeth Pratt.....	286	38
George, Richard J..........	118	37
Green, Annie...............	225	37
Gresh, Emily and Beniville F	27	39
Gresh, Samuel..............	154	39
Green, Dr. Charles H.......	88	39
Geisel, William J...........	269	38
Gregg, William S........... part of	378	39
Geyer, Samuel and Anna K..	377	39
Green, Mabel...............	161	37
George, Robert............. part of	81	35
Gebhardt, Maria	256	37
Gerber, Valentine E.........	441	39
Gerold, Magdalena	438	39
George, Henderson..........	447	37
Greathouse, Archie..........	452	37
Gillet, Horace S............	116	2
Givan, Mrs. Margaret........	37	2
Gillispie, Mrs. Jane.........	60	4

OWNERS' NAMES.	Lot No.	Section
Girard, Charles...................................	119	4
Griffith, Humphry, Heirs of.......................	10 and 11	12
Gibson, David.....................................	88	16
Ginz, Michael.............................part of	87	16
Gibson, Mary E....................................	158	16
Githrens, Griffith D...............................	36	17
Grimm, Wendell....................................	39	31
Girard, Sarah J...................................	147	27
Gillet, Samuel T..................................	16	4
Gilliland, Ezra T..........................part of	17	23
Gibbons, Arthur E.................................	35	32
Gibbs, William P...........................part of	129	2
Griffith, W. C....................................	81	32
Gill, Sarah J..............................part of	280	32
Gilmore, Thomas H.................................	7	18
Gird, John.................................part of	93	33
Grimm, Pauline, Heirs of..........................	258	18
Gisler, Conrad.............................part of	257	32
Gibson, William...................................	8	34
Gillette, Philip G.........................part of	27	12
Gish, Abraham G...................................	88	38
Gibson, Thomas W...........................part of	111	38
Grieb, Christina..................................	3	38
Gillette, Anna....................................	174	35
Griffen, John J...................................	46	37
Gilgour, William..................................	96	37
Githens, Martha E.................................	113	36
Gill, Josephine...................................	93	37
Given, John A..............................part of	32	36
Gilmore, Elizabeth W..............................	75	37
Ginz, Lawrence, Benj. F., Andrew, Leilah, Lizzie and Walter..................................part of	15	38
Gimbel, George F..................................	18	39
Giger, Henry J....................................	147	37
Gibbons, Mary Ann.................................	287	39
Grimm, Fred J..............................part of	305	39
Grinsteiner, George...............................	282	37
Griswold, John N...........................part of	323	31

OWNERS' NAMES.	Lot No.	Section
Gilbert, Amelia Q .... part of	268	32
Goddard, Samuel........	28	5
Goth, Peter...	161	4
Groeshel, Charles....	131	4
Gorrell, A. W............ part of	147	2
Gordon, Jonathan W .... part of	119	2
Glover, Joseph N............	11	5
Goldsberry, Georgia B	65	2
Goll, Mrs. Elizabeth.........	13	4
Grooms, A. C...........	44	12
Goodnoe, Mrs. Ellen......	129	16
Goodwin, T. B..........	82	3
Groesh, John	136	16
Goodheart, Benjamin F. and Julia H..........	6	13
Gompf, Christopher	35	19
Grosman, William......	14	20
Gosney, R. M............ part of	30	9
Gordon, Martha.........	115	25
Groff, Abraham	29	21
Gossam, William H	93	25
Gogen, James .... part of	20	25
Gordon, Mrs. Mary.......	33	14
Groves, Mrs. Harriet J.......... part of	243	25
Goodwin, Marcia M. B........	173	31
Grotrop, George.........	62	32
Goepper, Susanna............	337	32
Gossett, Phoebe A....... part of	200	18
Grobe, Charles H........	73 and 85	18
Goodnecht, William	21	33
Grove, Benjamin	76	18
Goebel, William........	224	18
Grove, William C	175	34
Goul, Andrew......	362	32
Goodlet, James.....	369	32
Goode, Elizabeth......... sub 1	1	17
Grout, Charles S .... sub 1	9	20
Gothhardt, Henrietta Christina .... sub 3	8	20
Goodnought, John.......	202	35

CROWN HILL CEMETERY.

OWNERS' NAMES.	Lot No.	Section
Gordon, William S	158	35
Goetz, Barbara	40	37
Gorman, Louisa M .... part of	233	35
Gold, Samuel N	311	35
Goheen, Frank H	83	35
Goebler, Henry .... part of	232	35
Gross, George	228	35
Gompf, Fred	82	38
Goodwin, Lizzie	92	38
Grossman, Charles	80	37
Goebler, Philipena .... part of	232	35
Goetz, Louis .... part of	126	38
Groff, Emma	42	18
Grout, Charles S .... sub 3	9	20
Goble, William	18	37
Groschel, John H .... part of	270	38
Gosset, T. F. .... part of	38	15
Gordon, Margaret D .... part of	12	39
Groff, Nathan B. and John C	84	39
Goza, Augusta S	187	37
Gorsuch, Charles W. and Belle C .... part of	323	31
Gordon, Robert B	280	39
Golladay, Mrs. Mary A	322	39
Goth, Charles L. and William .... part of	119	37
Groves, Helen J. M.	203	37
Gossett, Wilson S .... part of	200	18
Groennert, Henry	161	39
Grothaus, John H	478	39
Gould, Homer S	476	39
Gustetter, Mrs. Margaret	9	16
Grubb, William C	63	20
Grund, William	99	31
Gruenert, Rosa .... part of	152	27
Gunneman, Benjamin	63 and 64	32
Guthrie, Anderson P. .... part of	291	32
Grunewald, Henry and Sophia	181	18
Grund, George	36	18
Gustin, Lewis Q	257 and 259	18

OWNERS' NAMES.	Lot No.	Section
Guthrie, Francis A...............................	86	34
Gruenert, John H................................	39	4
Gruella, Thomas M. and Richard B...............	213	35
Guymon, Prestley................................	224	35
Guston, John .... part of	282	35
Guy, Sylvester M .... part of	47	38
Gudgel, David E......................... part of	340	35
Gutzwiller, Rosa	48	37
Gustin, Robert H........................ part of	78	19
Grummann, Julius	261	32
Guenther, Julius	10	39
Guth, Rudolph...................................	232	37
Guth, Edward	346	39
Guntz, Fred	430	39
Hanch, Jacob....................................	33	1
Hanna, John L...................................	131	2
Hayden, J. J....................................	8	5
Hartman, Matthew .... part of	27	7
Haynes, Philip...................................	61	5
Haughey, T. P. .... part of	2	6
Hammel, Andy	168	4
Hamlin, Carlin...................................	149	4
Harrison, Alfred .... part of	4	7
Harrison, John C. S...................... part of	4	7
Harkness, John	15	1
Hall, George Q	46	5
Hamlin, L. H....................................	129	4
Hardesty, E. J...................................	79	2
Haugh, B. F. and J. R...........................	30 and 31	8
Hannaman, William .... part of	28	6
Harbison, Robert................................	176	4
Hay, Lawrence G. and W. H......................	88	5
Hahn, Henry....................................	48	5
Harrison, Temple C	36	4
Hand, Levi S....................................	80	2
Haskell, G. A	110	2
Hamilton, T. D. .... part of	58	3
Hale, Henry J .... part of	129	2

CROWN HILL CEMETERY.

OWNERS' NAMES.		Lot No.	Section
Hapenny, Mary E. T.		81	4
Hawkins, John P.		55	1
Hammond, Abram A.		111	2
Hare, Marcus L.		21	12
Haerle, William.		18	16
Hall, Mrs. Sarah L.	part of	14	13
Hamilton, John E. and Samuel A.		35	15
Harmening, Harman		37	16
Hamilton, F. W. and others		4	11
Hamilton, William H.		58	17
Hack, John V.		21	17
Hartman, Charles		53	19
Hall, Hector H.	part of	82	3
Harmening, Christian.		38	16
Hanna, Samuel C.		52	13
Hanson, Mads		32	20
Harth, Matthus	part of	18	15
Harting, Henry and Engle		47	15
Hart, T. J.		21	21
Hardin, Albert G.		2	9
Habeny, Henry, Heirs of.	part of	29	12
Harris, Ruth		58	21
Hasson, James.	part of	47	3
Habig, Charles.	part of	146	25
Haslep, Isaiah D.		30	14
Hathaway, Solomon P.		85	25
Harris, David.		75	25
Harrison, Sarah H		42	31
Hawkins, R. O.		207	25
Harper, Jefferson.		9	31
Hart, Sarah.		116	31
Hazzard, David		81	27
Hauck, John.	part of	2	3
Hall, Mrs. Lena R		154	27
Hanbrich, Adam.		79	31
Harper, John W	part of	40	7
Harmeyer, G. F.		139	27
Hammond, Upton J		52	14

CROWN HILL CEMETERY.

OWNERS' NAMES.		Lot No.	Section
Hart, Thomas John......		195	31
Haueison, William	part of	36	3
Harcourt, Daniel W	part of	242	31
Harris, H. D	part of	242	31
Harmes, Charles E	part of	287	31
Harsch, Frederick.......		2	32
Hambright, Joseph	part of	264	32
Harmaning, William H	part of	336	31
Harmaning, Henry............	part of	336	31
Harris, Mrs. Louisa		45	32
Harlan, Mrs. Mary B..........		3	32
Hay, George...........		10 and 11	32
Harvey, Dr. Thomas B	part of	49	3
Harding, Mrs. Julia C		226	31
Hackman, Clara		36 and 37	32
Hamilton, William G...........		298	32
Harvey, Martha E., Heirs of		145	32
Hamilton, Lucinda Jane		297	32
Hartman, Charles F.................		24, 25, 31 and 32	18
Harrison, Thomas................		34	18
Harding, Matilda C	part of	75	21
Hancock, Benjamin F	part of	239	25
Harwood, William H...........		40	33
Haug, Catharine		131	18
Hall, Isaac N...........	part of	113	16
Hardacre, John		120	33
Haynes, Charles	part of	254	25
Hacker, Thomas S	part of	248	25
Harris, Marcus L...........	part of	158	27
Hanway, Samuel...........		190	27
Hall, Charles E...........	part of	255	25
Hanneman, John F. and Theodore H..............		22	34
Hayden, John C. and Emma L		56	33
Hancock, William		189	27
Hays, Anna L..............		115	34
Haymond, Mary M..............		132	34
Hartman, Philipina..............		43	34
Hazelrigg, Albert W..............		141	34

MAIN ENTRANCE—INSIDE VIEW

OWNERS' NAMES.	Lot No.	Section
Hawkins, Edward	189	34
Hansing, Ellinore	10	34
Hawk, Clark J........................ part of	169	34
Harrison, Theodore F.	21	34
Halstead, Charles M	194	34
Hannah, Alexander M	14	29
Hasely, Charles R	57	34
Hauser, Annie	316	18
Harrison, Lawsenia B. W	156	34
Hartman, Herman....................... part of	253	25
Hanna, Henry Hugh.................. part of	1	12
Harrington, Henry W	199	18
Hamilton, George W. and Myrta........ part of	303	32
Hawk, Joseph A	163	33
Hancock, John	195	35
Hamilton, Anna	29	35
Haffield, Calvin........................ part of	113	35
Hardwick, John, Heirs of................ sub 9	25	20
Hall, Lizzie A. and Sadie H............ part of	246	35
Hart, John	276	35
Hacker, Eliza A	124	35
Hansing, Henry..................... part of	66	33
Hasseld, Bettie	191	35
Hall, William H	247	35
Harris, Edward	188	35
Hadley, Joel W................. part of sub 2	64	13
Hamilton, Margaret.............. part of sub 2	64	13
Harmes, Theodore W	45	37
Hamilton, Mary...................... part of	225	35
Hauss, Philip Jacob	60	15
Hagan, Andrew	345	32
Hahn, John........................ part of	82	35
Hacker, Ashey P..................... part of	36	36
Haldeman, Park and Kinsie	302	35
Hagerhorst, William	261	35
Harper, James W.................... part of	81	33
Halpin, Martin H	83	36
Hawley, Channey H	56	38

CROWN HILL CEMETERY.

OWNERS' NAMES.	Lot No.	Section
Haughey, Schuyler C............... part of	2	6
Hammond, George .... part of	329	35
Hatton, Elmaza..... .... part of	53	38
Hall, Sarah L......................	81	38
Hahn, Mary L................... part of	34	34
Hays, Benjamin F..................	10	38
Hardie, William .... part of	59	13
Hammond, Martha F................	156	36
Habich, Albert C...................	125	38
Hanshaw, Mrs. Lee D .... part of	42	25
Hazen, Annie T...................	86	31
Hatton, John M................ part of	160	38
Hamilton, John	87	14
Halford, Elijah W.............. part of	75	14
Hartman, Charles.................	158	38
Haar, John	4	18
Hall, John.......................	133	37
Haskins, Elizabeth................	63	37
Harvey, Charles W.................	240	36
Hawkins, Epha A............... part of	74	37
Harseim, Robert G.................	58	36
Hamm, John, Jr .... part of	355	38
Harvey, Marcus P..................	298	35
Hampton, Wm. W. and Ida A........ part of	5	38
Hahn, Edward A. and Nettie........	36	39
Hagedorn, Henry	213	36
Haugh, Stephen .... part of	113	35
Hagelskamp, Richard .... part of	311	38
Harrison, Benjamin	57	13
Hazelrigg, Scott F.................	294	38
Habich, Mark.....................	243	37
Hardy, James D...................	229	39
Harris, Lena.....................	151	39
Hack, Laura, Louisa and Marguerite....	198	39
Hayes, Joseph G	16	37
Hady, James B....................	196	39
Habich, Carl.....................	101	39
Hartley, Benjamin W...............	164	39

OWNERS' NAMES.	Lot No.	Section
Hall, Rose E.	250	37
Hall, Lavinia A.	251	37
Hall, Joseph B.	283	39
Haffner, Emma F. .... part of	301	39
Hanson, Alice M. .... part of	308	38
Harding, Robert N., Jr	285	37
Haller, Herbert G. .... part of	167	36
Hazzard, David	448	39
Hafner, Catherine	292	37
Hawkins, Jennie .... part of	331	37
Hammond, Anna K	249	39
Haltmeyer, Maria	163	37
Haag, Melissa B	263	36
Haag, Louisa	86	39
Hamilton, James H.	303	37
Hancock, Charles E. .... part of	65	39
Hayes, George .... part of	186	39
Hahn, Louis	301	37
Harting, Henry and Louisa	422	39
Haynes, Rachel .... part of	423	39
Harmon, Matthew H	312	37
Haffner, Emma F. .... part of	393	39
Haubold, William E.	342	37
Handy, Harvey .... part of	496	39
Haas, George J .... part of	448	37
Hereth, John C	68	3
Helm, John .... part of	34	3
Hendricks, A. W.	5	1
Henderson, W	6	1
Hedges, Isaac L.	70	3
Hedges, Elijah	51	4
Hess, Casper	140	16
Heiner, Anna B.	40	17
Hetselgesser, Samuel and Lucien W.	5 and 17	17
Henderson, James	126	4
Hermann, George	78	20
Heinrichs, C. E.	64	20
Hepp, John K	47	20

CROWN HILL CEMETERY.

OWNERS' NAMES.	Lot No.	Section
Hedges, Cynthia A	5	6
Henderson, Alexander C	13 and 14	7
Hein, John R	11	7
Helms, Henry .... part of	12	7
Heine, Henry	10	7
Heckman, Christopher	8 and 9	7
Herron, F. M	34	2
Helms, Thomas M .... part of	36	7
Hesse, Henry D	13, 14, 16, 17, 18	8
Helwig, Charles .... part of	152	2
Helton, Mrs. Kate	82	2
Hessong, John J	154	2
Heller, R. J	15	7
Hedlund, John	63	7
Helmich, John	45 and 53	4
Heinbuch, George H	66	3
Henry, Maxwell B	2	4
Heitkam, John	9	17
Herren, Samuel .... part of	26	19
Hess, Frederick	123	32
Heiser, Henry	46	32
Hervey, Lamertine B .... part of	201	25
Herrlich, Herman	247	32
Hetherington, Benjamin F ..... part of	43	17
Heavin, Minerva	125	32
Hendricks, Thomas A	2	20
Heuston, Joel	92	32
Henderson, Melissa B	16	32
Henry, William and Jacob	10	18
Henderson, Charles E	110	18
Henry, William	52	18
Hervey, James W .... part of	256	25
Herpick, John	169	18
Heid, Fred .... part of	288	32
Hermann, Jacob	150	33
Heindel, Ida M	200	18
Herider, William C .... part of	158	27
Heath, William H	213	18

OWNERS' NAMES.	Lot No.	Section
Helming, Herman	166	33
Heller, James E. (admr. of estate of Alex. Adair)	292	18
Herron, Alexander .... part of	238	25
Helfer, Andrew A. and Edward T. .... part of	257	32
Heistand, Mary E.	282	18
Hensley, John H. and William A. .... part of	34	34
Hedrick, Henry	106	34
Herron, Frances E. and Alexander P.	94	34
Heiskell, Elizabeth J .... part of	5	3
Healy, Mary and Margaret .... part of	119	16
Hermann, Magdalena	334	35
Heiner, Mrs. Sophia	39	35
Heiner, Fred A	41	35
Heiney, Mary Ann and George ...... part of	32	35
Heinlein, Catherine and John ...... part of	20	33
Herndon, Lucy J .... part of	197	35
Hessong, Martin L	102	35
Hellyer, Lewis E. .... part of	272	35
Helmick, John	270	35
Heckman, William and Christian	14	38
Hermann, John	327	35
Hess, Conrad	46	38
Helbing, John	93	38
Hensley, John H .... part of	266	36
Hedderich, Peter	145	38
Herrington, Isaac H	55	36
Heizer, George Samuel	136	38
Hedge, Sarah A. .... part of	81	35
Hedges, William H	176	38
Helfrich, Adam	215	38
Hereth, George L. and Lucy A	207	38
Heim, Anna	60	37
Henchen, William H	202	38
Hendershott, Daniel J .... part of	322	38
Hesse, Sadie .... part of	91	37
Heine, Charles	330	38
Heiskell, Margaret .... part of	13	36
Hess, Casper	236	36

CROWN HILL CEMETERY.

OWNERS' NAMES.		Lot No.	Section
Herrman, Gustave L	part of	35	21
Herdrich, Charles		324	38
Heier, Frederick F		101	36
Hensley, Thomas F		39	39
Heston, Millie A		190	37
Hellman, Charles		146	39
Held, Emelia A		120	39
Hereth, J. George		199	36
Heizer, David F		160	36
Helm, Joseph		449	39
Hess, Herbert R	part of	64	14
Henninger, Edward, Sr	part of	12	38
Herr, Ida		276	37
Herig, John H		160	37
Helm, Adam Henry	part of	44	13
Hertzler, Elias M		314	37
Herriott, Juliette I	part of	47	12
Heath, Keziah A		298	37
Henry, Ella B	part of	220	39
Heiser, Edward M	part of	186	35
Henderson, Sarah		98	39
Heiser, Conrad		383	39
Helfer, Clarissa		422	37
Heizer, Cyrus C	part of	361	39
Hereth, Charles E	part of	295	39
Hildebrand, J. S		22	3
Hill, George W		52	5
Hines, Cyrus C		1	7
Hinkley, David J		26	1
Hill, James		7	1
Hinesley, William	part of	6	8
Hinesley, Andrew J		123	2
Hilkenbach, William		73	16
Hildebrand, Jacob S		93	4
Hill, Nathan		41	17
Hill, John Frances		90	20
Hipwell, William		37	20
Hickman, William	part of	34	17

OWNERS' NAMES.	Lot No.	Section
Hitchcock, Rachel...	6	25
Hinckley, William H...	72	25
Hill, James B..	1	23
Hildebrand, H. W...	144	25
Hill, B. F... part of	77	27
Hillyard, George W............................... part of	26	19
Hibben, Bernard Natal......................................	232	32
Hild, William..	245	32
Hillman, William, Jr. and Henry C. F................	283	31
Hitt, Maria J... part of	74	14
Hild, August, Heirs of.......................................	107	32
Highstreet, John..	69	33
Hill, Ralph...	159	27
Hinsch, Mary E...................................... part of	315	32
Hitz, George..	172	32
Hirschman, Jacob C.............................. part of	101	33
Hilton, James Wesley.......................................	17	34
Hindel, William..................................... part of	45	15
Hillman, Frederica................................ part of	335	35
Hilker, Frederica...	156	33
Hild, Henry P..	238	35
Hill, James V. T..	160	35
Hicks, Mary S...	72	36
Hill, Jeannette W..	162	38
Hillman, Sophia..	206	38
Hill, Richard...	94	36
Hindman, Michael M..	34	39
Hine, Mrs. Elizabeth...	5	19
Hickey, Helen and Joanna..................... part of	10	33
Higgason, William T., Heirs of.........................	145	37
Hixson, Walter B..	147	39
Hisey, Allen..	205	39
Higgins, Adah L..	170	39
Hill, William F. and Albert................................	175	37
Hine, Charles A..	310	37
Hines, Charles A.................................... part of	299	39
Highland, Sarah E................................. part of	296	39
Hilt, Daniel C..	272	35

OWNERS' NAMES.	Lot No.	Section
Holmes, W. C.	49 and 50	1
Hoss, G. W.	30	5
Hohlt, William	153	2
Hord, Oscar B .... part of	6	12
Hodgson, I.	26	3
Holliday, John H	39	7
Holliday, William J	24	8
Hooker, E. M. B. .... part of	58	4
Hoover, William H .... part of	80	15
Hopper, Lewis M	191	16
Hohl, C. G. .... part of	7	3
Hogland, Mrs. Nancy............. part of	106	16
Holler, E. Theodore	130	16
Hobart, Miss Lucretia	48	19
Hoover, Samuel C.	102	15
Houck, Martha .... part of	38	14
Homan, Anna M................... part of	40	19
Howe, Louisa, Jennie and Belle ... part of	81	14
Hoffman, Louis T.	53	17
Holloway, Mrs. John M.	26	20
Hosman, John W .... part of	16	21
Householder, John .... part of	26	9
Holle, H. C	52	19
Hoshour, Samuel K	36	9
Hofmeister, Nicholas	98	16
Hornaday, Isaiah.	96	16
Howes, Henry	166	25
Hoppe, John W.	82	25
Holbrook, Mariel H .... part of	155	2
Hogeland, Israel	3	31
Hoffmeyer, Christina	42	27
Hoover, Jacob B	141	27
Hopkins, Aurelia.	44	31
Howell, John W. and Thomas F .... part of	59	27
Howard, Samuel A	160	31
Holden, Emeline	92	31
Howie, William W................. part of	63	27
Hough, Mrs. Mary E	66	31

CROWN HILL CEMETERY.

OWNERS' NAMES.		Lot No.	Section
Holweg, Louis	part of	53	22
Holt, John F	part of	15	13
Hornaday, Thomas B		313	31
Hogshire, Samuel H		166	27
Hough, E. D	part of	210	25
Hohlt, Henry		206	31
Hohlt, William	part of	210	32
Holman, Milton C		85	32
Homburg, Mary C		113	27
Hoover, Elizabeth		219	32
Hollingsworth, Henry C		119	32
Hornberger, Andreas		234	31
Horning, Mrs. Fredericka		50	18
Howard Sarah F		327	32
Holliday, Rev. Fernandes C		185	27
Hohlt, Henry C		22	18
Hoffmeyer, Rebecca	part of	338	32
Hoffner, Luke		14	18
Hoyt, Harriet		28	33
Holland, Eliza J		14	11
Hoogland, Herman A		222	18
Hodson, Joseph		67	33
Howe, Mrs. Anna E		165	18
Holle, Christina	part of	69	17
Howard, Susan Ann		54	34
Hoffman, Lizzie		304	18
Howell, Lucy J		195	34
Holler, Mrs. Augusta		208	34
Hogshire, Mary E		231	25
Hoffman, Pearllena		157	34
Holzwarth, Caroline		17	33
Holland, Effie Catherine	sub 3	82	17
Hobbs, Martha A	sub 7	71	20
Holloway, John	part of	37	23
Howe, James L		24	35
Hosbrook, Daniel B	part of	102	27
Howard, Elizabeth		212	35
Holler, Delilah		17	38

CROWN HILL CEMETERY.

OWNERS' NAMES.	Lot No.	Section
Homuth, Frederick	347	35
Hosbrook, Harry .... part of	332	31
Hogeland, Joseph R	100	38
Howe, Daniel W	53	36
Hodges, Ambrose .... part of	111	38
Hoffman, Albert	127	38
Howden, Alice J	108	38
Hoff, Sarah .... part of	120	38
Hoshour, Edward S .... part of	182	38
Horner, David H .... part of	9	15
Holland, Theodore F	83	33
Holton, Winfred B	19	36
Holcombe, Harriet B	22	21
Holman, John A., Guardian	62	37
Hofmann, George and Minnie .... part of	382	32
Holle, Henry F. W	92	37
Hoover, Abraham L .... part of	159	32
Howe, Elizabeth E	235	36
Hoskins, Anna .... part of	194	38
Hoffman, Nancy Christiana	307	38
Holland, John H .... part of	284	38
Hoffman, Charles H	85	14
Hofmann, Catherine Eliza	149	38
Holmes, James	136	31
Howlett, Edward C .... part of	67	19
Hohlt, C. H .... part of	63	17
Hollingsworth, Zeph	19	39
Holloway, Charles E .... part of	26	14
Hofmann, Adaline and Otto	20	39
Hoskinson, Amanda L	242	37
Howard, Patrick L	112	37
Hotz, George, Jr .... part of	74	21
Hoskins, Charity	184	37
Hoffmann, John A. and Mary A .... part of	165	38
Hollenberry, Ella	140	39
Horning, John C	100	39
Holland, William A. and Calvin R	181	37
Hollingsworth, Elizabet A .... part of	159	36

CROWN HILL CEMETERY.

OWNERS' NAMES.	Lot No.	Section
Hoehner, Wilhelmina	177	39
Horne, John	360	37
Holle, Margaret	324	39
Howell, Susie	14	37
Holladay, Arthur .... part of	200	36
Howland, Desdemona Harrison ...... part of	4	7
Holler, Augusta .... part of	8	38
Holmes, Charles B .... part of	135	36
Howard, Lewis N	62	5
Hohn, George	252	37
Holle, Fred. W .... part of	69	17
Hoeltke, Caroline M	339	37
Hockersmith, Henry .... part of	268	39
Hockett, Frank M .... part of	456	39
Hole, Mary .... part of	487	39
Hollis, Hellen .... part of	501	39
Hoefgen, John .... part of	206	36
Hobart, William .... part of	502	39
Hornshu, Charles F	363	35
Hollowell, Matilda	252	38
Howe, Aaron B .... part of	291	39
Holle, Louis	78 and 79	16
Hoffman, Max .... part of	423	39
Hower, Laura C	527	39
Honnold, James L .... part of	81	39
Hoogland, Joseph and George W	424	39
Horney, Solomon C	429	37
Hubbard, William S	64	1
Hume, James M	16	2
Huey, M. S	27	5
Hunt, M. A. H .... part of	147	2
Hull, A .... part of	105	4
Hunt, Ann Eliza	44	2
Hunt, Charles C .... part of	6	3
Hunt, P. G. C .... part of	27	12
Hutchinson, David	56	15
Hutton, George	68	20
Hulsman, Alexander	91	17

OWNERS' NAMES.	Lot No.	Section
Hugo, Henry A.	28	20
Human, John	69	25
Hutchison, H. H. .... part of	70	21
Hunt, Martha	91	25
Hukreider, Ernst	145	4
Hughes, James	305	18
Hufford, George W	295	31
Hutchinson, Mrs. L. V	120	27
Hunt, Sarah C	246	32
Hussey, John R. and Mary B .... part of	58	13
Hugo, Charlotte	276	32
Husbands, W. M .... part of	188	32
Huffer, James M .... part of	184	27
Huey, Oscar L.	191	34
Hubbard, Monroe .... part of	138	33
Hunt, Lee and Eva	222	32
Hubbartt, James	133	34
Hussey, Thomas	130	34
Hudson, Albert G	313	18
Hubbell, Samuel R .... part of	28	3
Hust, George C	37	33
Hufnall, John A .... part of	170	36
Hutton, Eliza Jane	39	37
Huntington, Angelina C	286	35
Hunter, John M	356	35
Hutchins, Mary E .... part of	2	12
Huffington, Agnes M. and Abel C.	342	35
Hunter, Harry	28	36
Hubbartt, Richard .... part of	192	38
Hull, John H. and Granville H .... part of	87	36
Hutchings, Dalphon .... part of	182	38
Huggins, Thomas	1	3
Hughes, David C. and Isham	38	39
Huber, Francis J	297	38
Hugg, Martin M. and John A	264	36
Hugo, Elizabeth	171	39
Huntington, Martha	180	36
Hunter, Silas .... part of	305	39

OWNERS' NAMES.	Lot No.	Section
Hukreide, Henry Rudolph	387	39
Hudson, James W	262	37
Hunter, James T	310	39
Hurshman, Emma F	480	39
Hyde, N. A	64	7
Hyatt, Mary E	307	18
Hyde, Rev. Marshall B	85	38
Hyatt, John	78	34
Ingraham, John P. S	109	4
Ilg, George	282	31
Isensee, Albert ... part of	170	4
Insley, Ellis	49 and 50	5
Ingels, Joseph	59	21
Isensee, John F	23	27
Idler, Clinton	165	31
Ingersoll, Chas. H., Martha S. and Mary ... part of	38	7
Ireland, William H	225	32
Iske, Charles	182	34
Innes, Philip, Heirs of	340	37
Irick, William C	34	5
Iliff, Mrs. Mary M	99	4
Indiana Institute for Education of the Blind	30 and 31	7
Ihndriss, John	48	20
Inglis, John	97	25
Irick, William	76	25
Indianapolis German Protestant Orphan Association	49 and 53	31
Indianapolis Orphan's Asylum	50	31
Indianapolis Asylum for Friendless Women	51	31
Indianapolis Home for Friendless Colored Children	52	31
Irwin, Rollin C ... part of	106	16
Indianapolis Typographical Union, No. 1	1 and 2	25
Indianapolis Typographical Union, No. 1	109	37
Indianapolis Reform School for Girls' and Woman's Prison	110	37
Irish, Frank	270	37
Isgrigg, James A	308	39
Ivin, Albert	550	39
Inlow, John W ... part of	50	14

CROWN HILL CEMETERY.

OWNERS' NAMES.		Lot No.	Section
Ioor, John, Charles and Walter	part of	147	2
Izor, Albert		66	39
Jameson, P. H.		18	6
Jasper, Mina		53	16
Jacks, Mary L		44	20
Jackson, John		47	31
Jacobs, Charles P	part of	3	5
Jacquemine, Mrs. Odilie		174	25
Jaehrling, John P		31	31
James, Michael C		104	31
Jackson, Henry H		201	31
James, Ann Elizabeth	part of	266	31
Jameson, Lydia and Henry		104	27
Jackson, William N	part of	5	13
Jacobs, John		296	18
Jackson, Walter H	sub 15	58	20
Jay, Elijah		34	35
Jans, William		307	35
Jacobs, John	part of	82	35
Jaynes, Aaron H		104	38
Jackson, William J	part of	328	35
Jacobi, Mary	part of	77	38
Jasper, Herman		177	37
Jacobs, Sarah		257	37
Jacobi, August		203	36
Jackson Ellis B	part of	361	39
Jenison, Harriet T		5	3
Jenkins, A. W. and E. H	part of	31	3
Jennings, John		25 and 26	15
Jeffras, William		14	25
Jenkins, James		35	27
Jennings, George		207	32
Jenkins, John		40	34
Jencks, Rev. Joseph S	part of	239	25
Jessup, John W		114	35
Jenkins, Alfred		43	35
Jenkins, Lydia T		20	36
Jenkins, John		295	37

OWNERS' NAMES.	Lot No.	Section
Jenson, John	336	37
Jenson, Andrea	337	37
Jenson, August	335	37
Jenkins, Dennis H	108	39
Jeffries, Henry A	336	39
Jines, John R sub 2	85	20
Jillson, William M	50	29
Jordan, Lewis part of	28	8
Jones, Spicer part of	42	7
Johnson, Mentor S	133	4
Johnson, Charles L. F.	149	2
Jones, Aquilla	1	1
Jordan, John	46	1
Johnson, Elizabeth E. and Isabella M	19	2
Johnson, John F	44	1
Jones, Eliza J part of	25	16
Jones, Mary E	2	13
Jones, Robert A	188	16
Jones, Caroline F part of	47	12
Johnson, Mrs. Fannie part of	58	15
Johnson, R. D	174	16
Johnson, George W	16	19
Jones, Aquilla, Jr	9	13
Johnson, William, J part of	57	15
Johnson, Samuel A part of	57	15
Jones, Julia A., Elizabeth, Sarah, Ada and Andrew	44	15
John, Charles part of	66 and 73	15
Jones, J. W	60	21
Johnson, Martha C	38	25
Joachimi, Julius part of	150	25
Johnson, Lydia B. and James A part of	149	25
Johnson, S. F	79	25
Jordan, Harriet J	227	25
Johnson, Isabella	12	27
Johnson, Edward T	49	14
Johnson, John J part of	225	25
Johnson, William M part of	225	25
Johnson, David part of	224	25

CROWN HILL CEMETERY.

OWNERS' NAMES.	Lot No.	Section
Johnson, William S............part of	223	25
Johnson, Jesse B......................	222	25
Johnson, Tom L.............part of	20	23
Johnson, Mary E......................	123	31
Jones, Stephen D.....................	215	25
Johnson, Mrs. Mary...................	18	31
Jones, Amanda A............part of	75	27
Johnson, Catherine C., Melissa E. and Eli M....part of	74	21
Jordan, Dan S........................	300	32
Jones, John L........................	299	32
Johnson, James, Jr..........part of	83	21
Johnson, James, Sr., Heirs of....part of	83	21
Johnson, William.....................	137	32
Jones, Ralph H.......................	108	18
Johnson, Elmira L....................	238	32
Jones, Elizabeth.....................	3	18
Jones, Lewis...............part of	314	32
Jones, Nancy J.......................	32	33
Johnson, Julia Noble.................	94	27
Joiner, Joseph.......................	223	18
Jones, Rachel........................	29	33
Johnson, Thomas E..........part of	195	27
Johnson, Sylvester and Eudorus M.....	167	32
Job, M. G. Olivia..........part of	74	21
Johnson, Mary Annie..................	284 and 298	18
Jones, Mrs. Eliza J........part of	136	27
Jones, Margaret F....................	49	34
Johnson, Elizabeth.........part of	253	25
Jordan, Arthur.............part of	228	25
Jordan, William Riley......part of	253	25
Johnson, William and Louisa..........	112	35
Jolly, Maggie J......................	111	35
Johnson, Marquis L...................	100	35
Johnson, William K...................	30	35
Johnson, William C...................	278	35
Johns, Hiram A., and others...part of	157	35
Johnson, Gertrude..........part of	180	35
Jordan, Annie B......................	249	35

CROWN HILL CEMETERY.

OWNERS' NAMES.	Lot No.	Section
Jones, Alice	264	35
Johnson, Theodore .... part of	102	27
Johnson, Henry A. .... part of	102	27
Jones, Lewis C. and Sarah E.	70	19
John, Bertha	230	35
Johnson, Louis H	60	38
Jones, John R	62	4
Jones, John T.	325	35
Jones, Harriet D	122	38
Johnson, Joseph C.	106	38
Johnson, Elizabeth A ..... part of	232	25
Johnson, Frederick C ..... part of	3	20
Johnson, Millie	47	37
Johnson, Samuel T .... part of	387	38
Jones, Thomas E.	32	37
Jones, John and Hester C .... part of	23	35
Johnson, James C .... part of	208	31
Johnson, Callie .... part of	12	39
Jones, Mrs. Lou	274	18
Johnson, Alexander	173	37
Johnson, Sidney H .... part of	169	36
Jose, Herman C .... part of	219	39
Jordan, Joseph H., Mordecai, Wright S. and Barclay .... part of	129	39
Johnson, Ella .... part of	226	39
Jones, Willis D	41	4
Johnson, Clara R .... part of	35	39
Johnson, Samuel L.	277	37
Jones, Ella .... part of	356	39
Jonas, Minnie and William F	218	39
Johnson, Samuel O.	296	37
Jones, Wm. M. .... part of	371	38
Johnson, Nancy	324	37
Johnson, Henry F.	375	37
Johnson, Joseph R	436	39
Judson, Charles E. .... part of	175	4
Julian, John W .... part of	74	21
Julian, Esther J	187	32

OWNERS' NAMES.	Lot No.	Section
Julian, George W............... part of	196	27
Judd, Thomas.................. part of	42	34
Judson, Martha B...............	82	37
Jungclaus, William P........... part of	229	25
Justice, John Q................	136	39
Krauss, Jacob..................	21 and 22	5
Kappes, J. H...................	20	8
Kahle, Samuel F............... part of	155	2
Kares, Joseph..................	162	4
Krause, Reinhold...............	104	16
Kramer, William............... part of	109	16
Kalb, Henry, Sr................	56	17
Kramer, Andrew................	56	19
Klasing, Charles............... part of	87	19
Kantman, Francis.............. part of	79	19
Kramer, William H.............	1	27
Kaiser, William................	51	27
Kraft, John F.................. part of	95	16
Knannlein, Annie...............	74	31
Knauf, Adam...................	30	31
Krafthoefer, Elizabeth..........	144	31
Krag, William A............... part of	49	3
Kampf, John B................. part of	2	17
Kaylor, William H............. part of	170	32
Kautsky, Wenzel................	79	17
Kaiser, Louisa.................	302	18
Kaufman, Moritz............... part of	161	27
Knapp, Jerome B............... sub 5	25	20
Kaufman, Simon O.............. part of	23	35
Kahl, Charles..................	140	33
Kalb, Mary A.................. part of	143	35
Klanke, William F............. part of	50	35
Karrman, Julius................	159	35
Kraas, Wilhelm................. part of	329	35
Krabbe, John...................	179	35
Kattman, Ernst................. part of	63	17
Kamps, Frank G................	281	35
Kalb, Laura...................	338	35

OWNERS' NAMES.	Lot No.	Section
Kahle, Frederick C.	87	38
Kassebaum, John C., Heirs of	77	36
Kay, Joseph	322	35
Kaufman, Frank .... part of	164	35
Kalton, Henry	364	38
Karle, Christian	215	36
Kaley, Henry L.	30	37
Klausman, Henry	42	39
Kappes, William P. .... part of	77	14
Krauss, Emma C. .... part of	108	15
Krauss, Charles .... part of	108	15
Krauss, Christian	108	37
Kattau, William .... part of	114	39
Kayne, Jennie	308	37
Katharine Home for Aged Women	416	37
Kemper, John M	32	1
Kerr, Joseph	49	2
Kelley, Mrs. J. S.	173	4
Keesee, William N	103	4
Ketcham, John I.	54	7
Knefler, Fred .... part of	22	8
Kregelo, David	100	14
Kregelo, Mrs. Mary A	83	2
Kealing, Peter .... part of	12	12
Kendrick, W. H. .... part of	37	7
Kleine, Frederick .... part of	84	16
Kemp, Benjamin J	32	19
Keller, William P. .... part of	53	15
Kellogg, Mrs. Margaret E	17	15
Kelley, Lewis L	39	15
Keevers, John H	77	15
Klefker, Henry	59	19
Kersey, Oliver	3	9
Kerkhoff, Frederick .... part of	45	14
Keating, John .... part of	150	25
Kreutzer, John	49	25
Keely, William, Sr.	140	25
Kelshew, John	13	27

OWNERS' NAMES.		Lot No.	Section
Kersting, Benjamin	part of	187	25
Kepple, Martin		187	31
Keafer, John	part of	19	31
Kemker, Charles H		137	31
Krentler, Frederick C	part of	307	31
Keely, John S		252	32
Kleppfer, Anna R		96	32
Kershaw, Joshua D		251	31
Kreider, Reuben G		184	32
Kennedy, J. Walter		286	32
Kregelo, Charles E	part of	97	14
Kreitlein, A. G	part of	282	32
Kees, Hiram		62	33
Keay, William F	part of	238	25
Keely, Henry S	part of	64	14
Kremser, Annie		145	18
Keepers, Mrs. Florence J		247	18
Kennedy, William and John	part of	54	33
Keepers, John		239	18
Keers, Elizabeth, and George W		169	33
Knefler, Dan W		68	34
Kenyon, Kate A		159	34
Kerr, Mattie	part of	204	34
Klein, Michael		315	18
Keller, Robert F. H		94	16
Kreis, Anna Mary	part of	7	3
Kensler, John	part of	170	36
Kleiner, Caroline	part of	2	23
Kellermeyer, Anthony Frederick William		93	35
Klein, Nicholas	part of	229	35
Kelpin, Louisa Johanna		352	32
Kern, Elizabeth	part of	82	20
Kettler, John H		52	38
Keller, Henry		45	38
Ketterhenry, William		89	38
Keehn, Hiram W		105	15
Keeler, John I		6	37
Keller, Robert H	part of	3	20

CROWN HILL CEMETERY.

OWNERS' NAMES.		Lot No.	Section
Kleinschmidt, Henry	part of	111	27
Kehrer, Louisa		151	38
Kemp, Curtis H	part of	98	38
Kenney, Catherine		94	37
Keller, Zachariah P. and Geo. J	part of	212	36
Keller, Charles F		125	37
Kremiller, Caroline		149	37
Krebs, Reinhard	part of	29	39
Keeman, Marquis		30	39
Krentler, Engle		279	38
Kerr, Charles G		21	39
Kepple, John		93	36
Kettenbach, Henry		151	2
Kerfoot, L. B	part of	95	15
Ketcham, John H		85	39
Klein, Jacob	part of	262	36
Kessler, Mary A		46	36
Keller, William H		390	39
Kreitlein, Andrew G	part of	282	32
Kendall, Martha E		365	37
Kneale, William C	part of	378	39
Kennedy, Robert J		322	37
Kenyon, Hannah E		253	37
Kern, Ann M	part of	44	39
Kendall, Mary		389	39
Kellogg, Edwin P		126	39
Kempfer, Isaac N		258	39
Kendall, Sylvester W		292	39
Kendrick, Robert L		307	37
Ketcham, Laura Robson	part of	409 and 410	37
Kerkhoff, Mary		302	37
Klein, Barbara		423	37
Kirk, D. A		67	4
Kitchen and Bradley		29 and 30	6
Kiger, John		130	2
Kinder, Maria	part of	41	3
King, Edward		3	7
Keifer, Augustus		65	5

OWNERS' NAMES.	Lot No.	Section
Knight, John	54	3
Kingman, Nelson	156	2
Kline, Frederick	83	15
Kiser, A .... part of	57	17
Kistner, Catherine	81	16
King, Jacob .... part of	47	19
Kindler, Margaretta .... part of	15	20
Kissell, Frederick .... part of	46, 74	16
Kiefer, Jacob .... part of	99	15
Kinbrough, Isaac	80	19
Kindelburger, W. H	27	25
Knight, J. M .... part of	86 and 87	17
King, A. H	21	27
Kitzmiller, William	32	27
King, William S .... part of	153	31
Kidd, John	213	25
King, Mary .... part of	84	27
Kief, Michael C .... part of	144	27
Kirby, Nahum Wellington	148	31
Kritsch, William A	19	32
Kingsley, Adriel S. and Harriet F	111	32
Kistner, Rosina	49	22
Kiefer, Philip E	199	25
Kipp, Robert and Albrecht	62	14
Kirlin, James	206	32
Kline, George W	146	32
King, David	43 and 60	18
Kistner, Emma	304	31
Kirkpatrick, William T .... part of	182	27
Kline, Edwin J	236	18
Klinsmith, William	98	18
Klingensmith, Israel	148	18
Kimber, Abraham	202	34
King, Cornelius, Heirs of	338	31
King, Nettie I.	7	34
Knippenberg, Henry .... part of	21	23
Kinder, Wesley .... sub 11	58	20
King, John W	59	35

CROWN HILL CEMETERY.

OWNERS' NAMES.	Lot No.	Section
Kingsley, Charles E............ sub 1	41	20
Kingsley, Royal S .... part of	145	33
Krieger, Christina................	153	35
Knight, J. Newton .... part of	50	35
Kise, Elisha S .... sub 6	8	20
Krieger, John, Henry, George........ part of	8	35
Kirkwood, Adam	75	17
Kimble, T. V................	8	2
King, James W .... part of	81	33
Klingensmith, Isaiah L........	125	35
Kriel, Charles W........	177	38
Kinklin, Richard .... part of	190	38
Kline, Mrs. John G. and Esther........	163	38
Kile, Philip H........	159	38
Kindig, Henry I........ part of	87	36
Krieger, Alberta	129	37
Kimple, John N	135	37
King, William L........	158	32
Kise, John W........ part of	68	19
Klingstein, Emma........	55	39
Knight, George A........	95	14
Kiley, Rebecca J........ part of	346	38
Kingsbury, Nancy........	219	36
Kinnan, Minerva .... part of	224	37
Kirkwood, John A	72	33
Klingensmith, Ruben........	222	39
Kinney, Horace E	265	36
Klines, Edwin J .... part of	248	39
King, Eli	481	39
Kimball, Howard	73	39
Knickerbacker, David B .... part of	74	14
Kiel, Charles L........	437	39
Knight, Charles H	86	14
Kimble, Georgia A........	80	27
Koch, H. H. and Mrs. J. H........	32	15
Kolthoff, Frederick........	143	16
Kolwes, F. W	68	17
Koehler, William .... part of	103	16

OWNERS' NAMES.	Lot No.	Section
Kothe, William	20	15
Knowlton, Stephen	33	17
Knodle, Mrs. Elizabeth C	58	19
Koehring, Bernhard	86	19
Koller, Charles ... part of	39	21
Koeninger, George	17	27
Koch, Thomas	37	27
Koehler, Catherine ... part of	4	17
Knoelle, Rosa	83	31
Kotteman, William ... part of	318	31
Kopp, Albert F	63	14
Kolb, Frederick Wm. and Wm. Frederick	347	32
Kortepeter, Louisa ... sub 1	85	17
Kropp, Jacob ... sub 7	85	20
Koechert, Max P	176	35
Kolling, Christina	104	33
Kord, Frederick	117	35
Koch, George	217	35
Korn, Elizabeth	209	34
Kortepeter, William	89	35
Kohnle, Henry E. and Mary	301	35
Koeniger, John M ... part of	6	38
Koller, Mary E	126	35
Koch, Louisa Mary Sophia	42	36
Koster, Kate	148	38
Koepke, Louisa	153	38
Kothe, George ... part of	109	15
Koch, Simon	92	36
Kollmann, Elizabeth	51	37
Koebrich, Nicholas ... part of	207	39
Knotts, Elizabeth C	152	39
Knox, George L	201	39
Koeppen, John G	210	39
Koppen, John	266	39
Kokemiller, Malinda	343	39
Kopp, William H	345	37
Kruger, Joseph	49	2
Kunkle, Henry and Charles	180	16

CROWN HILL CEMETERY.

OWNERS' NAMES.	Lot No.	Section
Kruger, Henry .... part of	48	15
Kuhn, William F	71	15
Kuhn, Charles J	68	15
Kunkleman, Rev. J. A	33	25
Klusmann, Louis	26	25
Kunkleman, Margaret	70	17
Krug, G. C.	148	25
Kuerst, Henry	309	31
Kurtz, John G .... part of	133	27
Kruse, Henry .... part of	266	32
Kuester, Mary Lisette .... part of	118	34
Krueger, Frank	155	34
Kuechler, Louis .... part of	87	5
Kuhn, Charles J	22	37
Kurts, Hilpat	124	37
Kruger, Chris L	178	36
Kuntz, Martin C	321	38
Kuetemeier, Charles .... part of	11	3
Kruse, Henry F	323	39
Kuechler, Jacob	283	37
Lauer, Charles	59	1
Laird, J. P	138	4
Laird, W. H .... part of	63	5
Lawrence, A. V .... part of	70	2
Langsdale, Joshua M. W	86	2
Landis, Mrs. Ann C	99	2
Langsenkamp, William .... part of	6	3
Landers, Franklin	28	12
Layman, D. W	14	3
Law, Stephen	66	17
Larink, Mrs. H	45	17
Langford, Whitten S	21	20
Lawrence, Henry	75	15
Lahmann, William .... part of	42	15
Lay, George F .... part of	11	25
Lancaster, G. W	37	21
Landis, Milton M	10	29
Landers, Jackson and John	22	23

Owners' Names	Lot No.	Section
Labarth, Mary A.	44	25
Lang, Frederick........................ part of	48	25
Langley, S. D. C.	169	25
Lamb, Robert N.	22	15
Laatz, Henry........................... part of	49	27
Laird, Charles P.	25	31
Lang, Louis	60	2
Larger, James E....................... part of	56	27
Lang, Charles.	16	31
Langbein, Amelia.	188	25
Lang, George........................... part of	15	20
Langenberg, Henry W.	174	27
Langhorne, Barbara E., Barbara and Lucy N	131 and 132	32
Larger, Jerome........................ part of	38	7
Lauer, John B.	130	32
Lang, William.	185	32
La Forte, Mary Ann.	188	18
Latham, Charles and Henry	22	6
Larsen, Jens.	44	18
Lawsen, Peter.	175	32
Laakmann, Frederick	94	33
Lange, Leonhard.	41	18
Lane, John A........................... part of	238	25
Lamotte, Charles F.	122	33
Lane, Elanor R........................ part of	103	35
La Fountaine, Sarah.	178	35
Landis, William F. and Harry K	92	35
Lange, Frank A....................... part of	85	35
Lanktree, James W.................. part of	2	12
Lake, Martha.......................... part of	18	25
Laycock, William H	71	36
Lawrie, John	135	27
Lange, Henrietta D	56	36
Laing, Samuel......................... part of	387	38
Laux, Joseph, Heirs of	41	12
Laughlin, Caroline	209	37
Lammert, Fred.	224	39
Lawrence, Henry W.	260	36

OWNERS' NAMES.	Lot No.	Section
Lake, William................................part of	304	39
Laube, Louisa M................................	373	39
Laycock, Henrietta C.........................part of	301	39
Lackey, Frank....................................	240	39
Lafeber, Hattie...................................	321	37
Laycock, Sarah E...............................part of	399	39
Laboyteaux, Maud..............................	278	37
Langsdale, George J...........................part of	76	14
Lee, M. G...	66	5
Leach, Jesse C....................................	76	2
Lesh, Mrs. Isabel A.............................	122	2
Lewis, Walton W................................	196	16
Lensmann, Henry..............................part of	52	16
Lentz, William....................................	11	19
Leonard, Stoughton G.........................	44	19
Lewis, Sarah J....................................	16	20
Lemons, William................................part of	74	20
Lemon, John B....................................	50	20
Lehritter, Conrad................................	18	21
Lentz, Christian F...............................	25	19
Lenox, L. L..part of	20	25
Lehritter, Matthias..............................	130	25
Leeds, George.....................................	58	25
Leonard, J. R......................................	9	27
Legg, Benjamin F................................	4	31
Lewellen, Richard...............................	312	31
Lechene, Eugenia................................	65 and 66	32
Lewis, Catharine M...........................part of	38	13
Leck, Robert M...................................	97 and 124	32
Lee, Drusilla......................................	209	32
Lee, Mary J. T....................................	203	32
Leonard, Merritt E..............................	11	18
Lewis, Charles S. and Adaline P............part of	38	13
Learned, Ophelia................................	69	18
Lewis, John W....................................	78	18
Leachman, John T...............................	180	27
Lee, Edward.......................................	104	18
Lenkhardt, Christian...........................	174	18

OWNERS' NAMES.		Lot No.	Section
Leser, John.	part of	165	33
Lester, Jacob W.		161	18
Lee, Thomas G.		27	34
Leachman, Eliza.		128	34
Leach, Eliza.		288	18
Lemen, William E.	sub 2	81	17
Lenker, John and Michael.		115	35
Lewald, Philip A.		4	33
Lehr, John G.		98	35
Lee, William E.		5	16
Lewis, Edwin R.	part of	58	13
Lewis, Lucinda	part of	204	18
Lee, Mary A.		208	35
Lee, Mary L.		23	37
Lee, Amanda M.		90	36
Lehr, Philip.		42	38
Lee, Caroline		164	4
Lee, Oliver B.		67	36
Lemoine, Josephine.	part of	233	25
Lehr, Elizabeth.		83	38
Lewis, Charles E.		62	38
Lewis, William T.	part of	294	35
Lewis, Frank D. and Anna D.		73	36
Leffingwell, Artemas		196	38
Lehr, Katharine.		6	36
Lemmon, Isaac D.	part of	362	35
Leas, Clara Francis.		50	39
Ledford, Jesse S.	part of	127	37
Leonie, Lawrence	part of	289	38
Lewis, Anna M		133	39
Ledig, Julius.	part of	300	38
Lefferson, Henry M.		384	38
Lee, Mrs. Jennie Jane		284	39
Lehr, Margaret	part of	340	39
Lehman, John, Heirs of.	part of	315	37
Leach, James M.		380	39
Levey, Annie M., Marshall T., M. Dunn and W. Charlesworth.		381	32

OWNERS' NAMES.	Lot No.	Section
Legg, Nancy Jane................................	424	37
Leedy, William H..............................	314	39
Lieber, Herman................................	70 and 71	5
Lingenfelter, William L.......................	91	2
Lintner, Amos H...............................	190	16
Litel, Josephus................................	54	15
Lindley, Calvin................................	32	25
Lines, James W.......................... part of	80	17
Lipp, Charles A......................... part of	126	25
Lipfert, Minnie................................	77	25
Linn, John F. and others	7	7
Liebrich, Frederica............................	18	27
Likert, George.................................	41	27
Lindemann, Frank .... part of	92	2
Lintner, Mrs. Annie E.........................	69	31
Lindley Anna..................................	254	31
Little, Annie	181	31
Lindemann, William M........................	220	31
Lister, Mary E.................................	190	32
Lippus, William .... part of	28	1
Linton, Charles J..............................	221	18
Lilly, Eli......................................	18	14
Libeau, Charles H....................... part of	16	34
Lingenfelter, Deliscus	4	34
Lighter, Mattie................................	317	18
Lightford, James G............................	244	35
Light, Dr. Robert C...........................	355	32
Lilly, Catharine...............................	11	29
Lister, John	52	35
Linn, Thomas B...............................	316	35
Litton, Preston	155	35
Little, John W., Edward W. and Samuel	130	35
Lilly, Virginia C........................ part of	275	35
Light, Arthur F................................	43	37
Little Sarah A.................................	250	35
Lively, Eliza A................................	218	35
Liebert, Minnie S..............................	68	38
Little, Adam	104	37

OWNERS' NAMES.	Lot No.	Section
Linder, Elizabeth .... part of	3	20
Liebrich, John F .... part of	111	27
Lindenbolt, Mary Bell .... part of	2	16
Lieber Albert.......................	17	14
Linus, Dauiel.......................	174	37
Lister, Mary E......................	503	39
Lowe, Mary W .... part of	24	7
Love, Gen'l John................... part of	9	12
Louden, Mrs. Lucy..................	13	2
Louden, Mrs. H. L..................	40	4
Locke, Erie and Josiah..............	124	2
Love, William .... part of	3	3
Loucks, James......................	68	2
Long, David D......................	48	3
Lowman, Nancy L., Heirs of	62	2
Loucks, William W .... part of	55	3
Locklayer, Aaron...................	36	19
Love, Samuel...................... part of	29	15
Long, Florence, Alice, Geo. S., Eva J., Rhoda B., Susie M. and James E................ part of	51	15
Lowe, James C..................... part of	85	19
Locke, William M...................	54	21
Lohrman, Conrad	19	25
Lowes, John W .... part of	155	25
Lloyd, Margaret S.................. part of	133	25
Loeper, Jacob W .... part of	163	25
Loftin, Sample.....................	138	27
Long, Joseph .... part of	223	25
Long, Henry C .... part of	15	23
Loomis, George B...................	73	14
Losey, William S	196	25
Loomis, Elanor	183	32
Loftin, Joseph......................	326	32
Logan, Rev'd John B................	163	27
Loehman, Charles...................	215	31
Long, Nicholas H...................	125	18
Lowe, Gabriel......................	273	18
Loutham, David K .... part of	13	3

OWNERS' NAMES.	Lot No.	Section
Long, William C. and Emma A.	232	18
Lounsberry, Benjamin F.	189	18
Long, Eli C.	50	34
Love, Shaw C. .... part of	42	34
Lowe, Nahum H. Jr. and Nahum H. Sr.	13	34
Lowder, Joseph .... sub 3	58	20
Lockwood, Charles W. .... sub 3	92	20
Lowes, Elizabeth	357	32
Loftin, Almon .... part of	350	32
Lovejoy, John H.	135	35
Logan, R. D. .... part of	17	1
Lodge, Laban L. .... part of	282	35
Loder, Hannah Ann	290	35
Loesche, Henry	293	35
Loncks, Margaret A. .... part of	86	20
Lloyd, Washington B. .... part of	133	25
Lockwood, Matthew A.	69	38
Low, Thomas	123	38
Lloyd, Rebecca A. .... part of	168	38
Long, Robert D.	258	32
Loy, David M. .... part of	171	35
Long, Drusilla F. .... part of	29	36
Love, James F.	61	36
Loftin, Unity	212	39
Lowe, William W.	245	39
Long, John B.	364	35
Loesche, Hermann	460	39
Lockwood, Mary F.	164	32
Long, Mrs. Cordelia	320	32
Lueders, Catharine and Sisters	42 and 43	4
Ludwig, Philip .... part of	18	15
Ludorff, Louis	60	25
Ludlum, J. E.	112 and 113	31
Luse, Catherine D.	261	18
Lubbe, Louisa .... sub 1	25	20
Luedemann, John F. .... part of	21	19
Lutz, Mary M	134	35
Ludlow, Jason C .... part of	29	17

CROWN HILL CEMETERY.

OWNERS' NAMES.		Lot No.	Section
Lutes, Robert P	part of	110	15
Lucus, Sarah J	part of	247	39
Ludwig Louis		318	37
Lyhand, C. C		132	16
Lyons, Mrs. Aurelia M	part of	15	21
Lynch, Michael	part of	257	25
Lytle, Lem O	sub 5	1	17
Lytle, Baltzer K	part of	351	32
Lynch, Augustus D	part of	74	14
Lybrand, Joseph E		349	32
Mathe, Fredericka A. C	part of	170	4
Martindale, E. B. and Emma		1	24
Mason, Stewart		45	2
Mayer, Charles		23	3
Mayhew, James N		9	6
Martin, L. R		23	8
Mahoney, John T		151	4
Marshall, C. H		20	1
Martin, William	part of	28	3
Mann, Daniel		19	4
Macauley, Daniel		53	1
Maufeld, George		82 and 83	5
Martindale, William	part of	6	3
Marsh, Henry B		15	12
Masson, Mrs. Eliza		46	4
Matlock, James M		62	16
Malone, Mrs. S. J		154	16
Magley, Jacob		178	16
Maxwell, J. M	part of	25	3
Mardick, Mary A		55	16
Marland, John		138	16
Makepeace, H. B	part of	113	16
Martin, Gilbert	part of	86	16
Marsee, Rebecca H	part of	62	7
Mathews, Mrs. Martha A		65	17
Machett, Robert M		13	17
Mason, Benjamin	part of	67	16
Maschmeier, William	part of	52	16

A LAWN EFFECT.

CROWN HILL CEMETERY.

OWNERS' NAMES.		Lot No.	Section
Manning, Mrs. Anna		38	17
Martin, Thomas		87	15
Masonic Burial Ground Association		46	13
Mason, James	part of	37	19
May, Henry		93	15
Martin, William H		51	20
Massey, Mary S	part of	60	1
Mason, Benjamin	part of	40	19
May, Sallie R	part of	24	20
Magill, Robert J		59	20
Matthews, Edward		92	17
Mankedick, Henry		49	19
Maas, Lewis		99	15
Marshall, Levi	part of	78	19
Mattill, Christian		96	25
Matthews, Martha		113	25
Mayer, Wilhelmina		31	27
May, John P	part of	173	25
Many, John B., Heirs of		212	25
Mahan, Kate C		142	27
Matthews, Mrs. Sophia S		17 and 32	31
Manly, George W		15 and 34	31
May, Edwin J		141	31
Maginnis, Sophia		65	27
Mann, Mary A	part of	87	31
May, Edwin F	part of	191	25
Mai, August		67	27
Mayo, Abbey R	part of	14	23
Maroney, Matthew J		110	32
Mansur, Amelia B		18	11
May, Christina	part of	210	32
Mayhew, Francis L		112	27
Mann, Samuel		41	32
Mangold, Frederick		32	32
Mays, Philip		72 and 73	32
Mayer, Naber F		313	32
Mauer, Elizabeth		136	32
Mahan, Eliza		201	18

CROWN HILL CEMETERY.

OWNERS' NAMES.	Lot No.	Section
Martin, Fredericka	203	38
Magel, Mrs. Anna Elizabeth	165	27
Madaris, Flora	68	18
Maguire, Charles .... part of	81	14
Manshardt, George	44	33
Maurice, John N	77	33
May, Mrs. Amanda	307	32
Marahman, Charles	166	31
Marshall, Firman	227 and 231	18
Madsen, Christian L. F .... part of	266	31
Martin, Joseph T	293	18
Mansur, Mrs. Hannah A .... part of	254	25
Mayer, John Gottlieb	53	34
Mast, Edward .... part of	128	33
Marshall, James H	138	34
Martin, Emil .... part of	118	34
Matzke, Julius	18	35
Maxwell, Charles D and Samuel A .... part of	27	8
Marshall, Caroline L .... part of	25	3
Martz, Henry K. and William H	1	33
Marshall Nathaniel F	239	35
Mahoney, Charles	38	35
Marks Caroline .... part of	33	35
Mattern, Mary A	9	37
May, Harry N	46	35
Marquis, Ebenezer .... part of	266	35
Matherson, Andrew	26	38
Marshall, David R	22	38
Martindale, George W	315	35
Mayer, John F	86	36
Magner, Jennie H	346	35
Mazelin, John B., Heirs of	105	38
Maddox, William R	128	38
Martin, James B	201	38
Mansfield, William H	347	38
Marquis, Eugene K	376	38
Mason, Mary J	24	33
Matheny, John .... part of	386	38

CROWN HILL CEMETERY.

OWNERS' NAMES.	Lot No.	Section
Matthews, John E.	59	36
Mast, Maggie C.	58	37
Martin, Rinhard C. L. ... part of	285	38
Mayer, Frank J. and Augusta L.	365	38
Malott, Volney T. ... part of	5	23
Macy, Mary A. ... part of	5	23
Matthews, Claude	38	9
Mather, Mary L. ... part of	118	32
Maxwell, Dr. Allison	23	36
Madden, Joseph	237	37
Manning, Hattie	113	37
Major, Stephen F.	176	25
Mann, Willis R.	114	37
Matkin, Isaac S.	295	38
Maxwell, Howard ... part of	196	36
Matthews, Elizabeth	127	39
Mather, Sarepta F. and Daniel	244	39
Martin, Elwood L.	302	39
Maloney, John	350	37
Madison, Erwin W.	327	37
Mathias, Jacob ... part of	62	13
Marsh, Joseph	270	39
Maillard, Marie	330	39
Martens, Herman	239	39
Marten, Grace	269	37
Matchett, Eliza A.	439	39
Martin, Rebecca J.	333	39
Maschmeyer, August	536	39
Merryman, Martha A.	68	4
Metzger, Alexander	68 and 69	5
Meyer, George F.	24	6
Merrill, Samuel	16	7
Meredith, Samuel C.	59	5
Meginnis, Mrs. Frances	53	3
Meier, Lewis	83	4
Messersmith, John ... part of	81	2
Meyer, Frederick	147	16
Meikel, Mary ... part of	7	16

OWNERS' NAMES.	Lot No.	Section
Means, Mrs. Thomas A.	69	20
Meikel, Mrs. Mary C.	10	11
Meurer, Albert E. ... part of	24	9
Metcalf, G. W. and J. S.	128	25
Metzner, Adolph	56	25
Mead, Mrs. L. C.	28	31
Melling, Charles	85	31
Meginnis, Thomas J.	277	31
Meredith, Mrs. Jane and Albert E.	296	31
Metzger, Charles	308	31
Meigs, Charles D., Jr. ... part of	263	31
Meigs, Charles D.	264	31
Meyer, William and John Henry	204	25
Meyers, Christian	211	31
Mefford, James. ... part of	150	32
Medert, Margaret	134	32
Mettler, Theresa	23	18
Meyers, Isaac	59	33
Meyers, John ... part of	1	20
Merritt, George	42	3
Meyers, James C ... part of	13	3
Mears, J. Ewing ... part of	14	13
Merrill, Hattie E.	295	18
Meigs, Mrs. Anna L.	158	34
Meyers, Jennie ... part of	253	25
Meyers, Flavious J. and Ellen ... part of	253	25
Meadows, John ... sub 2	25	20
Meyers, William ... sub 9	58	20
Meyer, Amelia ... sub 3	72	20
Meyer, Theodore	366	32
Meimberg, August	273	35
Mezger, John	29	38
Merithew, Leslie E.	113	38
Merrill, Isabella	186	38
Mercer, Jennie ... part of	166	38
Meredith, Richard O. ... part of	388	38
Meek, Mary E. ... part of	173	25
Merrill, John F	115	4

CROWN HILL CEMETERY.

OWNERS' NAMES.		Lot No.	Section
Mendenhall, J. B.	part of	28	17
Meeh, Herman	part of	288	32
Meyer, Christian F. G.	part of	7	36
Meredith, Sadie	part of	128	39
Meyers, Eliza J.	part of	304	39
Meyers, William E.		177	33
Merz, Sophia		272	37
Meier, Mary	part of	125	39
Meyer, Louis	part of	91	20
Metzger, Catharine	part of	63	16
Merz, Fred		357	39
Mendenhall, Elijah	part of	173	16
Metcalf, Arthur B.		260	37
Miller, Edward T.		57	3
Milender, W. B.		100	4
Middaugh, Miss Catharine		10	16
Miller, Mrs. Martha		65	16
Miller, John		15	17
Miller, Ernst		36	20
Mitchell, James C.	part of	81	20
Miller, N. C.	part of	13	9
Milner, Davis		20	21
Miller, Albert	part of	5	15
Miller, Gertrude M.		51	14
Miller, Jehu		5	27
Miller, Samuel		105	14
Miller, John	part of	87	27
Mittag, Fredericka		14	27
Miller, William H. H.	part of	89	14
Miles, R. R.		110	31
Miller, John W.		151	31
Mittay, Henry and Margaret		125	31
Mitchell, Simeon J.	part of	231 and 232	31
Miller, Harry S.	part of	139	31
Miller, Mark D.		81	31
Mintner, Albert		54	19
Mick, William E.	part of	21	14
Mitchell, Rose T.		86	32

OWNERS' NAMES.	Lot No.	Section
Miller, Frederick	64	21
Miller, William Henry	220	32
Miller, O. S. ....part of	153	31
Miench, Kasper	38	18
Mills, Julia A.	149	32
Millison, Alice J. ....part of	2	17
Miller, George W. ....part of	110	27
Mitchell, Annie N. ....part of	317	31
Miers, James Pratt	96 and 121	18
Minor, Benjamin B.	190	34
Mittee, Samuel E.	137	34
Minkner, August Henry William	52	34
Miller, Andrew J.	176	34
Milliken, Henry C.	164	18
Miller, Mrs. Dora R. ....part of	110	33
Mintner, Smith ....part of	112	33
Michael, Allen ....part of	341	32
Michael, Manuel ....part of	341	32
Miller, Caroline D.	280	35
Miller, Phoebe	283	35
Milliken, Emma	216	18
Mix, Lyman W.	47	35
Middlesworth, William	53	35
Miller, James P.	163	18
Miller, Rudolph	141	35
Miessen, Eliza M.	96	35
Mills, William ....part of	87 and 88	35
Miller, Anna C.	50	36
Miller, Adam D.	36	38
Miller, George ....part of	78	35
Miller, Nannie E.	71	37
Miller, Edward H.	94	38
Miller, Eliza A. ....part of	24	9
Miller, Reinhold A. ....part of	38	20
Michie, Albert	321	35
Miller, Isaac M.	128	37
Michelfelder, John G. ....part of	394	38
Miller, Nathan E.	155	38

CROWN HILL CEMETERY.

OWNERS' NAMES.	Lot No.	Section
Miller, Winfield W. H................................	30	36
Miller, Martha J............................... part of	156	38
Minter, Mary L......................................	22	36
Mitchell, Thomas W......................... part of	234	36
Mitchell, Pauline............................. part of	32	36
Minich, James A............................. part of	252	25
Miller, John H......................................	290	32
Miller, Hiram W....................................	340	31
Mitten, Louisa C....................................	16	39
Michel, Christian and Bertha.....................	163	39
Mitschrich, Herman................................	371	39
Miller, Henry F.....................................	396	39
Milholland, John A.................................	348	37
Mitchell, James L............................ part of	75	14
Miller, Frederick H................................	366	37
Mitchell, Louis C., Annie T. and Lyman A...........	489	39
Miller, John A......................................	108	25
Miller, Albert R....................................	15	39
Miller, Reinhold H.......................... part of	117	16
Miller, Albert S. and Nettie.......................	416	39
Mitzenberg, Mary..................................	325	37
Mitchell, Rebecca J................................	312	39
Morrison, W. H....................................	63, 66 and 68	1
Morris, Morris, Heirs of............................	1	6
Mottery, Ferdinand	63	3
Morse, A. C..	31	1
Moffitt, William....................................	36	6
Moss, Andrew......................................	65	4
Morrison, John J...................................	107	4
Mortland, A. M....................................	139	2
Moore, Charles P...................................	47	4
Mounts, Henry M..................................	66	2
Monroe, Felix T............................. part of	124	16
Morrell, Rachel	51	17
Moore, J. R................................. part of	38	15
Moody, Mrs. Clarissa........................ part of	71	3
Moore, Geo. W .... part of	45	19
Moesch, Mrs. Eliza.......................... part of	82	20

OWNERS' NAMES.	Lot No.	Section
Moores, Jessie R	17	21
Moore, John........................ part of	60	1
Moyer, Joseph...................... part of	53	21
Moore, Aaron	66	25
Montieth, Mrs. Mathias	56	21
Moore, Mrs. A. W................. part of	42	25
Mount, Mrs. Julia A.............. part of	83	25
Moore, Fanny S.	24	31
Morrison, James A................ part of	137	27
Morris, S. S.	192	31
Moses, Lucius W.	168	27
Morris, Mrs. Jennie	270	31
Morgan, Levi L.	13	32
Morris, Charles R	321	32
Mohs, William	196	32
Moore, Thomas C	155 and 182	18
Morgan, William F.	235	18
Monninger, Daniel	39	33
Mode, Elizabeth.................. part of	4	15
Moore, William H.	25	33
Moore, John and Sarah........... part of	171 and 174	32
Morrow, Wilson	193	27
Moorhouse, Albert	131	33
Moore, Josephine M	23	33
Mollenkopf, Samuel.............. part of	134	33
Montgomery, Mrs. Martha and Minnie........ part of	106	27
e, Henry	276	18
re, Robert E.	83	18
gan, Greenbury	137	18
orrell, Lewis H................... part of	6	7
Moore, Catharine	248	18
Moore, Silas H.	79	34
Montague, Sanford............... part of	10	22
Moore, James L.	45	34
Mohler, Samuel L.	148	33
Morris, Cyrus R. N	263	35
Monteeth, John	171	33
Monticue, Jesse B................. part of	7	35

OWNERS' NAMES.	Lot No.	Section
Moldthane, Albert Franz	5	33
Moore, Sarah A .... part of	92	27
Morris, Vierling K.	365	35
Monfourt, Moses .... part of	354	35
Moore, Sarah .... part of	129	27
Moore, Thomas C .... part of	25	35
Morton, Lucinda M.	37	9
Moriarty, Charles R .... part of	85	35
Morgan, Lawrence	101	37
Montgomery, Francis M. .... part of	234	25
Moore, Katharine A. and Joseph M	90	38
Moulton, John F .... part of	175	38
Moore, Jennie Ann	90	37
Morris, William, Nellie and Elizabeth ...... part of	116	37
Morey, Clara .... part of	22	21
Mount, Elmer M. .... part of	284	38
Morrow, Jennie B	338	38
Moss, Lewis	115	2
Moore, Thomas	133	2
Moore, Joseph A. .... part of	7	8
Mordaunt, Frederick S .... part of	86	20
Monroe, Jasper R. and Harry C	380	38
Morgan, Lewis	214	38
Moulton, Rodman J .... part of	35	39
Mowery, Alfred and Flora .... part of	7	39
Morgan, Belle	168	37
Moore, Henry	121	39
Moore, John W	132	39
Morand, John F. .... part of	322	31
Morgan, Mary .... part of	72	38
Morris, Griggsby	188	37
Moore, Ollie E .... part of	32	39
Moore, James H. and Thornton L.	135	39
Moore, Albert G. .... part of	86	16
Morse, William	248	38
Morrison, William H	18	29
Moore, Arminda C	83	39
Monninger, Conrad	339	39

CROWN HILL CEMETERY.

OWNERS' NAMES.		Lot No.	Section
Morgan, Benjamin F........	part of	192	38
Morris, William H....		410	39
Moore, Albert W....		275	39
Morris, Barbara........		278	39
Moorman, John A. Jr. and Calvin S........		307	39
Mount, Mrs. Frances L.......	part of	399	39
Moon, Virgil....		411	37
Moker, George W....		227	37
Moores, Charles W.......	part of	22	7
Moore, Jennie E.......	part of	141	39
Morgan, Benjamin M.......		515	39
Munson, David....		18	2
Munsell, Ezra....		26	4
Munsell, Henry....		37	4
Munson, Charles H....		75	3
Muecke, William....		145	16
Mussmann, Diedrick.......	part of	90	16
Murry, Mrs. Mercy....		63	19
Muhleman, Christian and Charles........		84	20
Muir, Mrs. Elizabeth....		30	13
Mueller, Mrs. Frederick........		29	13
Mueller, Jacob.......	part of	46	20
Mueller, Mary....		51	19
Munhall, L. W....		44	21
Mulholland, Caroline.......	part of	62	25
Mueller, John Adam.......		167	27
Mueller, Henry....		80	31
Murphy, Jane....		218	31
Mueller, John Fred....		277	32
Mustard, James....		321	31
Mueller, Margaret....		289	32
Murphy, Jonathan A.......		167 and 170	18
Muir, Henry W. and Mary A.......	part of	317	31
Muir, James W.......	part of	317	31
Murry, John H.......	part of	131	27
Mueller, John A. D.......	part of	11	3
Murphy, Patrick L....		132	35
Mugge, Herman....		183	35

OWNERS' NAMES.	Lot No.	Section
Mueller, Andrew J. .... part of	25	38
Murray, Richard	122	37
Mueller, Edward	339	31
Musgrave, Mrs. Sarah A.	77	20
Mueller, Mary B	139	39
Muehl, Siegmar	158	37
Mussmann, Anna E	172	16
Myers, Rosanna St. Clair	147	4
Myers, J. G	132	4
Myers, Christina B	34	21
Myers, James C .... part of	257	25
Myers, Levi	11	33
Myers, Mary and Henry	2	39
Myers, Jane C .... part of	308	38
Myers, Alice .... part of	32	39
McDonough, D. B.	10	2
McCarty, Margaret	71	1
McPeak, D. J.	165	4
McFarland, D. L. .... part of	7	6
McLaughlin, William H .... part of	41	3
McLain, Mary S	36	1
McIntire, Wm. O .... part of	177	4
McClure, Col. Daniel	4	2
McGaw, John A	38	2
McCarthy, Joseph F	26	2
McCurdy, G. W	39	2
McChesney, Jacob	29	8
McLaughlin, G. H .... part of	82	15
McClure, J. F. and J. H	130	4
McKenzie, William	166	4
McDonald, David, Heirs of .... part of	35 and 37	3
McOuat, Mrs. Janet S	1	13
McArthur, Mrs. Letitia	20	4
McClure, M. T.	125	2
McWhorter, William .... part of	30	12
McKeand, Mrs. Elizabeth	73	2
McIntyre, Mrs. Dilly	199	16
McClure, Jacob H	155	16

CROWN HILL CEMETERY.

OWNERS' NAMES.	Lot No.	Section
McVay, James	173	16
McDonald, Joseph E.	13	13
McCann, Mrs. S. D.	12	17
McCormick, Mrs. Lucinda	23	13
McDiarmid, Duncan	35	16
McCarty, Orin P.	56	20
McLain, John............ part of	10	9
McLaughlin, Elizabeth .... part of	82	15
McCurdy, William W. H	51	25
McGinnis, Geo. F............ part of	23	16
McCaw, Mrs. Maria	26	21
McNeely Elisha	89	17
McCarty, Mrs. Lucinda C.	15	11
McCord, Christina............ part of	217	25
McGinnis, William	126	27
McKay, Samuel and Emma	40	27
McMurry, James	171	27
McNabb, Stephen............ part of	217	25
McMillen, Samuel and Mary	202	31
McCauley, William	186	31
McVickers, A. W	67	19
McIntire, Mary E............ part of	195	27
McGinnes, James W. and James	78	27
McKinley, Hugh............ part of	219	25
McClintock, William H	260	32
McPheeters, Clark	48 and 49	32
McCray, Lucus	200	25
McClure, Alonzo	93 and 128	32
McClintock, Robert............ part of	294	32
McClintock, William............ part of	295	32
McLaughlin, Frank	40	31
McGahan, Fred L.	204	32
McMahan, Emma	217	31
McQuiddy, John W.	279	32
McManis, Mary	15	18
MacQuithey, Horace P.	226 and 208	18
McKnight, E. M	203	18
McIntire, Mrs. Elizabeth L............ part of	133	27

OWNERS' NAMES.		Lot No.	Section
McMurry, James	part of	195	27
McCune, Hiram B	part of	21	14
McNeely, John B		250	32
McMullen, Mrs. Ella A	part of	137	33
McLaughlin, Almira and Frank		214 and 218	18
McKibbins, George		128	18
McBride, William P		206	34
McNemar, William	part of	162 and 173	18
McLain, Joseph M		164	34
McClellan, Leonidas H	part of	135	33
McCullongh, William J	part of	111	33
McMillan, Sarah M		106	35
McMillan, Amanda		26	35
McGuire, Elizabeth		245	35
McBride, Charles S		151	33
McClellan, Finley	part of	305	35
McClintock, James H		77	35
McKiernan, Warren	part of	275	35
McFarland, Benjamin F		64	35
McCune, Mary E		102	37
McPherson, William M		306	35
McVey, Hugh O	part of	211	36
McClellan, Frances M. and George M		80	35
McCracken, Mary N		70	38
McCollin, John M		56	35
McCready, Benjamin F. and Mary H		242	35
McConney, N. I	part of	78	14
McDowell, Cincinnatus H		109	38
McDougal, Louisa S	part of	232	25
McKee, William		137	38
McCrea, Rollin H. (Administrator)		158	4
McCray, Samuel		54	37
McCord, Sarah E	part of	164	38
McMillen, William	part of	369	38
McDonough, John		349	38
McVey, Mamie S		31	36
McCain, John E. and Joseph H		329	38
McKay, Laura E		277	38

CROWN HILL CEMETERY.

OWNERS' NAMES.	Lot No.	Section
McWorkman, Willard	157	32
McCloskey, John H	48 and 49	39
McGannon, Orlando C	7	37
McGuire, Nancy .... part of	47	39
McChesney, Sarah	189	37
McDonald, Thomas W	156	39
McCoy, Celeste H .... part of	322	31
McKay, Horace .... part of	44	13
McWhinney, Elizabeth A .... part of	9	15
McKeen, Margaret .... part of	150	37
McElroy, Martha F	344	39
McClure, William J	392	39
McCullough, Jacob S	231	39
McKee, Robert S	16	14
McConnell, Thomas	107	39
McIlvain, Samuel H	198	31
McFarland, William	300	39
McLaughlin, Lieu R .... part of	186	18
McLaughlin, Olive F	297	37
McClure, Phlegon T. T	156	16
McCoy, John B .... part of	291	39
McArthur, Anna J	524	39
McNutt, George and Jennie	382	37
McLain, Dr. Liberty C	297	39
McGinnis, Charles J	500	39
McCullough, Emma .... part of	464	39
McCulloch, John .... part of	392	37
McCauley, Charles and Jane E	251	39
McAlpine, Alexander R .... part of	324	31
McLaughlin, Margaret	113	39
McGinnis, Mrs. Florence S .... part of	470	39
McMullen, Valentine S	471	39
Naltner, George Edward and Addie .... part of	4	21
Nading, Ruth W .... part of	183	18
Naegell, Laura B .... sub 7	58	20
Nash, George W	300	35
Nagel, August .... part of	152	38
Naltner, Mrs. Barbara .... part of	58	4

WINTER SCENE.

CROWN HILL CEMETERY.

OWNERS' NAMES.		Lot No.	Section
Nachtrieb, Margaret	part of	272	39
Navin, Mrs. Catherine		257	39
Nan Kervis, Charles	part of	43	17
Newman, Omar	part of	15	29
New, John C		4	8
Newcomb, H. C.		46	3
Nesbit, William T.		104	15
Newcomer, Dr. F. S.		5	13
Neighbors, Charles	part of	126	25
Neffle, Frederick		114	31
Nelson, Henry H., Heirs of		26	31
Nelson, Horatio L		11	31
Newton, William	part of	3	3
Neisler, Oscar L		233	31
Nesmith, James W	part of	169	31
Nesbit, J. A	part of	96	31
Newby, Columbus	part of	25	32
Newhouse, George		176	27
Negley, Calvin		217	32
Nelson, Elizabeth Ann	part of	284	32
Neeb, Charles		155	32
Nelson, Rev. Thomas A		96	14
New, Valentine		143	32
Newby, Frank S	part of	36	34
Neal, William	part of	10	22
Neerman, Christina		77	34
Neidling, Christina	part of	233	35
Nelson, Lewis C	part of	127	35
Nelson, James W	part of	127	35
Nesmith, Sarah E	part of	254	35
Neiger, Elizabeth		152	4
Newport, James G		74	38
Neal, Mrs. Lucretia	part of	232	25
Neighbors, Jeanette I	part of	340	35
New, Adelia		39	36
Neff, Laura, B	part of	24	19
Newton, Mariah S		12	36
Newman, John B		44	36

OWNERS' NAMES.		Lot No.	Section
Nees, Charles		142	37
Nessler, Frank		24	39
Nesbit, Joseph A	part of	64	2
Neesen, Henry	part of	5	39
Newton, Josephine E		149	36
Neville, Mrs. Annie		389	37
Nerge, Minnie	part of	125	39
Newby, Jacob L	part of	393	39
Nelson, Ella J	part of	298	38
Nealy, Wesley	part of	8	39
Needler, Clara E		99	39
Newby, Nathan		74	39
Neff, William E	(also pt. 529)	528	39
Neffle, George H	part of	352	39
Nicholas, Addison		22	4
Nicholson, David		157	2
Nicolai, Mrs. Fredricka	part of	141	4
Nicholas, Rachel G		33	15
Nicolai, Ernstine	part of	65	15
Nieman, Joseph and Elizabeth M		24	25
Nies, Louis		36 and 13	31
Niemeyer, Joseph and William W		14	31
Niemeyer, Henry	part of	209	25
Nickerson, Margaret		90	18
Nicholson, Jessie T		68	35
Nilius, Sybilla		227	35
Nieman, Henry	part of	34	3
Niermann, Henry		292	35
Niermann, William		291	35
Niehaus, Katherine		31	38
Nichols, Edwin		112	14
Niebergall, John		146	38
Niemeyer, Frederick		161	38
Nichols, Smith T		193	36
Niedhamer, Sarah J		56	39
Nicolai, Emma		30	32
Nicholson, Andrew J	part of	289	38
Niblack, William C	part of	44	13

OWNERS' NAMES.	Lot No.	Section
Nieman, Sarah C.	167	39
Niedlander, Adne	268	38
Nicholson, Sarah	65	38
Niemeyer, Frederick	39	16
Northway, John	171 and 172	4
Northway, George M	49	7
Noble, W. H. L	5	12
North, Myron part of	1	16
Norwood, George	1	4
Nolting, Charles part of	189	16
Noel, Samuel V. B. part of	5	7
Noe, A. J	19	9
Norwood, John L part of	8	21
Nordman, Frederick	65	25
Noble, Nancy M part of	24 and 25	21
Nowland, P. B. L. and E. R	118	27
Nottmeyer, Christian	138	31
North, Johanna	263	32
Nordyke, Addison H	285	31
Norton, Lester L	215	32
Noble, John C	95	27
Noe, Mrs. Hettie A. sub 8	25	20
Noelke, Frederick part of	2	15
Norman, Isaac H.	134	38
Norton, Lyman C	34	37
Norris, Martin V	1	39
Noffke, August	23	39
Nolter, Frank J	228	39
Noerr Frederick	387	37
Null, Sarah part of	7	16
Nutt, Sarah E. part of	197	35
Nutting, Ada E. part of	130	27
Nydam, Melville	247	37
Ohr, John H	50	7
Off, C. and G. and J	86	5
Off, George Philip	85	5
Ott, Anna	152	33
Ott, John part of	314	35

OWNERS' NAMES.		Lot No.	Section
Orsbach, Mrs. Louisa	part of	46	15
Oswald, Kate		275	18
Orman, Andrew		168	39
O'Harrow, John W	part of	354	39
O'Neal, Charlotte		15	15
Okey, Edward H		63	15
Overholzer, Mary E. and Louisa E		7	9
Overmeyer, Nelson F		5	25
Over, Ewald		211	25
Otte, William		97 and 124	31
Orme, Mrs. Catharine		193	31
Otter, William E		188	31
Ostermayer, Louis		117	32
O'Neill, James and John		248	31
Obermyer, Maria A		94	32
Owsley, Mrs. Chas. D. and William A		74	32
Oehler, Roman		79	33
Olsen, Olaf R		187	34
Orner, Mrs. Mary B		136	34
Ogle, Alfred M		58	14
Oberly, John		28	35
Olmstead, Harry W		284	35
Orner, Theodore F		131	35
Ogden, Horatio N	part of	87	36
Oberle, Bertha H		286	38
Oelschlager, Albert	part of	171	35
Owens, Benjamin F		145	2
Owsley, William H	part of	289	38
Owen, John S. and Emma		231	37
Overman, Elizabeth S		282	39
Overmeyer, Rosa C	part of	211	37
Ostermeyer, Mrs. Emma	part of	327	39
Olin, E. D		114	15
Oliver, John		60	32
Oliver, Hannah E		68	33
Owings, Nathaniel B		2	30
Orill, Benjamin P	part of	28	3
Oliver, Harriet M	part of	71	20

CROWN HILL CEMETERY.

OWNERS' NAMES.		Lot No.	Section
Oliver, Charles	part of	234	35
Obrist, Robert Henry		102	38
Oliver, Lillie May		67	37
Oliver, John W		350	38
Oliver, Thomas J		45	39
Oliver, Rezin R	part of	227	39
Oliver, Mrs. D. H		361	35
Osgood, J. R	part of	9	1
Osborn, Benjamin F		221	31
Osborn, Elizabeth	part of	58	3
Osgood, Mason J	part of	96	27
Osgood, Mary A		99	37
O'Connor, Charles and John, Jr		105	37
Otto, Albert C		276	39
Osburn, Dan M	part of	219	25
Oursler, Lafayette	part of	169	36
Outland, Cornelius	part of	129	39
Oddy, Tom		465	39
Pattison, W. A		15	6
Patterson, Mrs. Clement	part of	121	2
Parker, Mrs. Henrietta	part of	59	3
Parker, Mrs. C		47	2
Patterson, John P		27	7
Parry, Mrs. Mary		21	8
Pattison, E. G		45	7
Pfaff, W. A		25	12
Parker, J. F		63	2
Palmer, Mrs. Mary		42	16
Prange, Frederick		121	16
Pattison, W. T		47	7
Patterson, Samuel W	part of	12	3
Parker, W. G		9	19
Payne, General W		122	4
Parkman, Charles B	part of	27	6
Parry, Rodger		67	25
Pattison, Isaac N	part of	23	6
Pfaff, John W	part of	29	12
Partlow, William		317	32

OWNERS' NAMES.		Lot No.	Section
Paetz, Annie	part of	26	27
Painter, G. W	part of	33	21
Patton, W. A		10	31
Plank, Sabitha L		38	31
Pauli, Henry		143	31
Parmelee, John R		140	31
Pavey, Francis M	part of	149	27
Parmelee, William H	part of	6	8
Pattison, C. B		237	25
Prasee, Henry		179	32
Paul, Henry		334	32
Pratt, William B		188	27
Patterson, William A		210	18
Patterson, Andrew		98	33
Palmer, John		168	33
Paulisch, William		318	18
Patterson, Alonzo	sub 4	25	20
Plank, August H		149	35
Patton, Mary	part of	109	35
Paulsen, Carl		65	33
Parrish, Amanda A		35	33
Patterson, Elizabeth A	part of	208	31
Pratt, Joseph W		168	35
Pasch, Albert		185	35
Park, Lyzeldia E	part of	149	25
Payne, Mary	part of	28	3
Patterson, Grace	part of	225	35
Pause, Louis C	part of	163	32
Pascoe, Louisa		143	38
Palmer, Amelia A	part of	232	25
Parker, Charles J. W. and Thatcher W		97	36
Prange, Henry C. F	part of	121	37
Palmer, Harry B		143	37
Pauli, Bertha	part of	25	39
Pasch, Carl		22	39
Platt, Frances		170	37
Pfafflin, Lewis	part of	44	39
Paver, John M		139	36

CROWN HILL CEMETERY.

OWNERS' NAMES.		Lot No.	Section
Palmer, Margaret A	part of	173	39
Palmerton, Mrs. Allen H.		207	37
Paxton, Eva F	part of	252	35
Patterson, James		262	39
Paul, Frank L. and Joseph B	part of	181	36
Paff, Matthew H	part of	340	38
Prahm, Adolph F		388	39
Parrott, Horace and Burton E		128	27
Patterson, Thomas R		522	39
Paddock, Robert L	part of	268	32
Perine, P. R.	part of	20	2
Pentecost, Mahlon B.		61	3
Penn, Samuel		16	12
Phelps, Allen E.		17	4
Perrine, T. B. and Huldah J		127	2
Peck, William		125	16
Perry, John C		10	15
Pettit, A. H		56	5
Perhamus, John T.		33	20
Peele, Stanton J.		50	15
Pedlow, James C. and Robert J		9 and 10	25
Peak, Susanna		94	25
Preston, Alfred	part of	151	25
Perry, Joseph R		53	14
Peck, Mrs. Mary A		1	30
Peak, Kate L		116	25
Peck, Frances A		20	27
Peterson, Gottfred		34	27
Pearsoll, Mrs. Hannah		149	31
Pease, Charles O	part of	20	23
Pearson, Charles D. and Charles D., Jr		93	14
Pease, Frank H		73	27
Pellett, William A.		122	27
Perry, Janet	part of	63	27
Phelps, Anna J.	part of	42	20
Pfeiffer, Lizzie	part of	307	31
Perkins, Edward A	part of	69	27
Pfleger, Jane Mary		29	32

CROWN HILL CEMETERY.

OWNERS' NAMES.	Lot No.	Section
Peine, Mary	40	32
Peine, John Henry	5	32
Penn, Joseph	144	32
Peterson, John D	138	18
Pederson, Peter	59	18
Pearson, Ora part of	255	25
Petty, Ransom	217	18
Phelps, Mrs. Sarah M	131	34
Perdue, Rebecca	256	18
Pease, Catharine Ann	23	34
Peak, Benjamin J	63	34
Pendergast, Enos part of	234	25
Pleeschner, Charles	331	35
Perkins, Mary Emma part of	92	20
Peck, Mrs. Carrie S sub 3	85	17
Pressly, John T	249	25
Perry, Walter	147	35
Pfleger, Elizabeth part of	133	35
Peak, James, Thomas and Harriet part of	354	35
Preble, Glenwood part of	12	14
Pearce, Thomas Charles part of	61	14
Petery, Mary	4	38
Perkins, Samuel E part of	6	12
Peters, Rev. J. Christopher	201	32
Peters, John	74	36
Peters, Henry part of	362	35
Peterson, Sophia	29	37
Perry, James and William	342	38
Peachee, James F. and William M	53	37
Prentice, Frances	45	36
Peoples, Josephine	248	37
Pressel, Mary	154	37
Perkins, Ellsbury H	86	33
Pennington, Alfred	72	19
Perry, Mary E part of	77	3
Petet, Nancy	194	37
Pfeiffer, Bertha F	495	39
Peterson, Soren	445	37

OWNERS' NAMES.	Lot No.	Section
Pfleck, Elizabeth M	516	39
Pendleton, Ralph C. J	373	37
Pierce, Dr. Winslow S	18	3
Phipps, L. M .... part of	41	5
Phipps, Isaac N .... part of	35, 36 and 37	3
Pierson, L. W	47	5
Phipps, Isaac N .... part of	19	12
Phipps, Joseph B	20	12
Prinz, John D .... part of	80	16
Pigg, James M	30	17
Pinkerton, Marietta E	43	15
Price, Mrs. E. J .... part of	35	9
Phillips, C. S	66	14
Phillips, Hugh M	70	25
Pittman, G. S .... part of	56	27
Pierson, C. C .... part of	73	3
Pickerill, William N	63	31
Pierson, Sophronia	90	32
Pickerill, G. W	18	18
Pfirmann, Barbara	45 and 58	18
Phillips, Isaac H	181	27
Pinger, William R	105 and 112	18
Prigge, Henry	160 and 177	18
Price, Daniel M .... part of	74	34
Pringle, William W	76	34
Pfisterer, Peter	348 and 349	35
Phillips, Harry	69	35
Prindle, Cynthia	40	38
Pittman, Jennie	64	38
Pierson, John C .... part of	163	32
Phipps, William C .... part of	234	36
Phillips, James F	59	34
Pierson, Amanda A	171	37
Pritchard, Evan H	145	39
Piel, Henry W	182	37
Pintzke, Johan G .... part of	440	39
Potts, Charles	146	4
Porter, William M. and Rebecca	128	4

CROWN HILL CEMETERY.

OWNERS' NAMES.	Lot No.	Section
Porter, Omer T.	43	14
Power, Jacob B	61	19
Poe, John M	62	15
Pope, Abner	10, 11, 39 and 40	20
Probert, Samuel	19	20
Pohler, Henry........ part of	48	15
Porter, Albert G	92	14
Poindexter, Parrat	95	25
Pothast, Christian	88	25
Pottage, Benjamin, Heirs of	186	25
Plogsterth, Victor	178	25
Porter, Mrs. Sarah	147	31
Polster, Fred	174	31
Pollard, Allison........ part of	274	32
Pope, Wilkinson	108	32
Pollard, William........ part of	274	32
Porter, Beverly	113	32
Poulter, Elizabeth A	99	32
Pouder, Angeline........ part of	212	31
Pointer, Mary J	132	18
Porterfield, Henry D........ part of	116	33
Poindexter, Robert E	136 and 141	18
Powell, George W........ part of	81	2
Poirier, John B. and Sarah A	225 and 233	18
Popino, Joseph	159 and 178	18
Poulter, H. H.	270	18
Prosser, Hettie........ part of	113	33
Potts, Francis S., Heirs of	13	35
Potts, Clayton, Albert and George	313	35
Probst, William J........ part of	220	25
Prosser, Mary A	229	35
Poppie, Mary........ part of	351	32
Power, Margaret	337	35
Potter, Merritt A	79	36
Pope, Henry F	144	38
Potts, Clayton........ part of	126	38
Pool, James........ part of	5	20
Pope, Mrs. Johanna Coleman	71	3

OWNERS' NAMES.		Lot No.	Section
Potts, Mary F	part of	220	39
Pouder, Mrs. Frances Ann		412	39
Powell, Fleming		319	37
Porter, Jacob M	part of	334	39
Poole, James and Lillian	part of	182	16
Prough, Caroline		75	39
Porter, Sarah A	part of	14	15
Pursel, Susan		3	16
Pursell, Mrs. A. A		76	16
Pugh, Jesse		53	2
Pugh, William		88	15
Pugh, Isaac C	part of	293	31
Pflueger, Fred G		283	32
Purdy, Adeline		90	34
Pursell, Lida S		192	34
Pursell, Peter M		200	34
Pruuk, Hattie A	part of	1	35
Pumphrey, Mary O		299	35
Plummer, John T		129	38
Purviance, Harry B		174	38
Pugh, Frank J		117	37
Pursel, Mary Amanda		152	37
Putnam, Miss L. R	part of	59	3
Pyle, William L	part of	29 and 69	4
Pyle, John		18	5
Plymouth Church, Trustees of	part of	2	3
Pyle, Marshal J		110	34
Pye, Sallie C		373	32
Pryor, Martin P	part of	35	21
Quisenberry, Mrs. Clara	part of	45	16
Quinnell, Mrs. Rebecca		43	20
Queisser, Caroline		83	27
Queisser, Frank F		310	31
Quinnius, Augusta		64	18
Quineas, John G		234	18
Quigg, Clara M		71	35
Ray, James M		70	1
Ray, John W	part of	35 and 37	3

CROWN HILL CEMETERY.

OWNERS' NAMES.		Lot No.	Section
Randall, H. P.		158	2
Ramsey, John F.		32	12
Ratti, Francis A., Sr		16	17
Raab, Sebastian		135	16
Randolph, Emily F	part of	59	13
Rapp, F. J.		35	14
Rasemann, Fred		8	25
Rawzell, Samuel		78	25
Radcliffe, John O	part of	40	7
Rau, Mrs. Clara		70	31
Raible, Mrs. Minnie		161	31
Ransford, William P.		146	27
Rand, Frederick		3	2
Ransdell, Daniel M	part of	26	23
Raymond, Charles H.		148	27
Randall, Horace and Ella A		330	31
Raffensperger, Hiram C		119	27
Rapp, Magdalena	part of	152	27
Rafert, Henry		236	32
Rafert, Charles F	part of	56	1
Rains, Hiram		184 and 185	18
Radzie, Caroline		12	18
Ramsey, Walter L		204	31
Raugh, John		133	33
Rathert, William		315	31
Raeder, John		135 and 142	18
Raeder, William		134 and 143	18
Raper, George		20	34
Ranja, Ada		127	33
Raymond, Margaret S	part of	22	35
Raper, Elizabeth	sub 6	71	20
Rafert, Christopher F.		49	29
Rassmann, Emil C	part of	160	32
Ralph, William E		97	38
Rahe, Caroline C		138	38
Randall, Theodore A		57	36
Railsback, Charles	part of	252	25
Ramey, William L		102	36

OWNERS' NAMES.		Lot No.	Section
Ramsey, Albert B		238	37
Rahke, August		220	36
Ratcliffe, Irene	part of	65	39
Ramsey, Alexander L		385	39
Redmond, Mrs. Catherine		14	4
Reynolds, John	part of	45	3
Reinken, Albert, Jr	part of	27, 28 and 41	1
Reinken, Albert, Sr	part of	27, 28 and 41	1
Reinken, Henry	part of	27, 28 and 41	1
Reese, Henry C. J	part of	141	4
Reed, Anson T		63	4
Resener, C. F. and H. F		69	3
Reichwein, Philip		31	16
Reed, Mrs. E. R	part of	24	12
Revels, W. R		71	16
Reed, Mrs. W. R		42	17
Reiffel, A	part of	57	17
Reeve, Mrs. Sarah and Grace D	part of	34	15
Reed, B. F		49	17
Reagan, D. J	part of	30	20
Reich, Mrs. Rebecca C	part of	65	20
Reeves, Thomas		50	19
Reitz, Henry and Charles		76	21
Reynolds, C. H		68	25
Reinchild, John	part of	53	21
Read, Walter H		10	21
Renner, Christian	part of	105	25
Reynolds, Hannah		106	25
Reed, William	part of	171	25
Reynolds, W. B		78	31
Rentsch, Amelia	part of	163	25
Reger, William		127 and 128	31
Reuter, George		197	31
Reinhart, Peter J		194	31
Redmond, John F		170	31
Rentsch Mary	part of	6	3
Rebentisch, Henry		258	31
Redding, Jerry		87	32

CROWN HILL CEMETERY.

OWNERS' NAMES.		Lot No.	Section
Reagan, John		55	32
Reid, Johnston	part of	294 and 295	32
Reissner, Albert and Emelia		306	32
Redmond, Harriet		205	32
Reeves, Carey C	part of	189	25
Rees, Robert H	part of	337	31
Reynolds, John W	part of	183	25
Reichardt, Charles F	part of	130	33
Reeder, Eliza		39	34
Ream, Laura		242	25
Reading, Mary F		254	18
Reiffel, Martin		121	33
Reed, Andrew J		56	34
Regula, Sarah		279	18
Reibold, Louis		13	29
Reynolds, Sallie E	part of	33	33
Reynolds, Miles M	part of	33	33
Recker, Gottfreid		139	33
Reed, Enos B	part of	2	33
Reid, Mary E		142	34
Ressler, Charles L	sub 1	8	20
Reese, Ferdinandina	part of	53	22
Reno, Nancy	part of	36	35
Rees, Eliza Catherine		203	35
Reed, Daniel A		122	35
Revel, William W		173	33
Reinberg, Henry		206	35
Reyer, Henrietta C		7	33
Reynolds, William L		94	35
Reger, Frank		274	35
Reinhart, Philip	part of	129	31
Reams, Kate	part of	268	35
Renkert, Philip		262	35
Reeves, Frank J		99	38
Reed, Elizabeth		361	32
Reform School for Girls' and Woman's Prison		110	37
Reese, Clifton V		35	37
Reiffel, Charles	part of	4	20

RECEIVING VAULTS AND CHAPEL.

CROWN HILL CEMETERY.

OWNERS' NAMES.		Lot No.	Section
Reid, Adaline E. and George W.		147	38
Rentsch, Edward H., Jr.		208	38
Reese, Charles	part of	169	38
Reichardt, John	part of	204	38
Rebesberger, Henry and Kate S.	part of	7	3
Reynolds, Anna Bell	part of	119	34
Reifers, Herman	part of	343	38
Reeder, Ephraim C.		339	38
Remy, Allison C.	part of	37	23
Rehling, W. C., H. A. and C. H.		173	27
Record, William		28	13
Reisner, George A., Edna May and Horace G.	part of	158	36
Reis, Henry W.		203	39
Reddehase, Frederick	part of	176	39
Reveal, William O.	part of	154	36
Reveal, Annie E.	part of	154	36
Reynolds, Charles C.	part of	29	36
Rea, Samuel B., Henry S. and Thomas N.	part of	206	39
Rehme, John E.		157	37
Rehm, George H.	part of	90	17
Reagan, Amos W.		395	38
Reed, Edwin H.		441	37
Read, Melvina H.	part of	502	39
Reynolds, William E.	part of	295	39
Rescue Mission and Home of Indianapolis	part of	4	20
Richmond, Joseph S.		33	4
Richmond, N. P.	part of	12	1
Richards, K.		137	4
Ritzinger, J. B.		67	7
Riley, Mrs. W. H.		114	4
Richenbaugh, Mrs. Margaret		54	2
Rihl, Charles H.		17	12
Richter, Mrs. Adolphus J.		137	16
Richardson, Frank		105	16
Richardson, Benjamin A.		85	15
Riley, Benjamin F.	part of	12	3
Richter, F. B.	part of	24	17
Ripley, William I.		41	19

OWNERS' NAMES.	Lot No.	Section
Richardson, Harland	20	20
Riner, R. M.	98	15
Richmann, Charles	76	19
Richards, F. W.	73	20
Riedman, Henry	9	9
Richards, Edward N.	17	9
Riley, Eliza J., Heirs of............ part of	7	7
Rickard, Mrs. Emma J.	31	14
Rickerds, Thomas	118	25
Ridgway, Sarah B.............. part of	47	19
Riley, Mrs. Nancy	22	31
Richters, Henry	200	31
Rhinehold, Jacob	64	31
Ringer, John Q. A. .... part of	60	16
Ritter, E. F.	76	27
Ripley, Warwick H.............. part of	263	31
Rice, Martin H..... .... part of	36	3
Richter, Fred................. part of	117	27
Riechemeyer, Henry............. part of	267	32
Ricketts, Indiana C............. part of	15	13
Risner, Carl and Frederick	164	27
Richard, Verdilla E.	191	18
Riemenschnieter, H	71	33
Ritter, Levi..................... part of	192	27
Riddle, David	149	18
Richardson, D. H	272	18
Rieman, Charles	167	34
Rinner, Herman	69	34
Richter, William and Dora	19	33
Riebel, Frederick	144	33
Rippetoe, Elizabeth S............ sub 3	85	20
Rinehart, Martin L............. part of	350	32
Ridenour, Martha	59	29
Richardson, Stoughton K. and Nancy A	175	35
Ries, Conrad	20	38
Rich, William S................ part of	211	36
Richardson, Mary M.	98	38
Riley, John W	88	36

OWNERS' NAMES.

Name		Lot No.	Section
Rippeto, John A.	part of	168	38
Richter, Christina		86	38
Richenberg, Augusta W.	sub 8	85	20
Richardson, Mary F. and Joseph F.		50	37
Richardson, Joel F.		198	36
Richardson, Mary E.	part of	374	32
Richardson, Clara L.	part of	142	39
Richter, Dora H.	part of	18	33
Richter, Henry C.		13	33
Richardson, May	part of	128	39
Richards, Edward N.		34	9
Ritter, Christina		230	37
Rigg, Herbert L.		305	37
Ross, J. T.		140	4
Rhodes, John W.		136	4
Root, Deloss, Julia and Jerome B.	part of	25	6
Romerille, Charles E.		101	2
Robinson, Anna M.	part of	38	7
Rockwood, William O.	part of	27	6
Rhodius, Mrs. Marie		24	2
Root, Mrs. A.		143	2
Roe, Robert		128	2
Rowe, Samuel P.	part of	55	3
Ross, Alfred		104	4
Roos, Rowlena		26	16
Roberts, Joseph S.		13	16
Roberts, H. W.	part of	167 and 168	16
Rhodes, J. H.		146	16
Roth, Adam		46	17
Rooker, Rachel	part of	40	14
Rooker, Calvin F.		49	21
Robbins, Mrs. Charles J.	part of	40	19
Roesiner, Anthony		100	15
Rockwell, Rufus E.	part of	22	13
Robinson, John		55	20
Roback, A. G., H. H. and E. T.	part of	54	20
Rowe, William		12	21
Rozier, Rebecca		62	21

OWNERS' NAMES.	Lot No.	Section
Rose, Fieldon W..................... part of	147	25
Robinson, J. W..........................	61	25
Royster, Samuel.................. part of	47	14
Routier, Peter...........................	168	25
Rouse, Nancy E.........................	84	25
Robinson, Frederick M..................	107	25
Rodibaugh, Adam.......................	135	25
Rowe, Catharine........................	1	31
Robinson, Jerome.......................	28	27
Robertson, Samuel G....................	169	27
Rogers, Levi, Heirs of...................	136	31
Roberson, David J................ part of	224	25
Rowney, Emma..........................	93	16
Ross, James J...........................	159	31
Roesner, Charles........................	214	25
Rosenberg, John.................. part of	52	21
Roche, Patrick James....................	134	31
Ross, William...........................	294	31
Rowney, Annie..........................	276	31
Roller, Jacob............................	61	31
Rohner, Frank J.........................	265	32
Rothert, John H.........................	251	32
Rose, Sarah J...........................	38	32
Rodenberger, Mrs. Samuel...............	53 and 52	32
Roberts, Alabama.......................	271	32
Rorex, George A........................	120	32
Roberson, Lucy A.......................	91	32
Ross, Johnson H.................. part of	250	31
Root, Charles G................... part of	2	7
Robinson, Henry R. C.............. part of	2	17
Robinius, Mary M................. part of	319	32
Rodgers, Catherine......................	265	31
Roach, William J.................. part of	320	31
Rouse, R. R.............................	114	18
Robertson, Webb........................	47	33
Rogers, James N........................	97 and 120	18
Robertson, William and Roxanna.........	127 and 150	18
Roetter, George.........................	263	18

OWNERS' NAMES.

Name		Lot No.	Section
Rosch, Sophie	part of	165	33
Robinson, Mrs. Louisa O		180	34
Roesener, Henry C. F		25	34
Rhoads, Charles W. and Arthur		60	34
Rosengarten, Leon F		98	34
Ross, Frank		192	18
Robinson, James A		235	32
Roberson, Charles, Sr., and Charles, Jr.	part of	256	25
Rodgers, Effie	sub 6	92	20
Rost, August		48	35
Roepke, Helena	part of	72	3
Roberts, Isabella L	part of	57	27
Rosengarten, Henry and Mary		9	35
Rowe, George E		170	35
Rommel, Mary	part of	319	32
Robinson, Mary K		84	35
Rollins, Ella	part of	240	25
Royce, James T		68	36
Roy, Herman J		357	35
Robinson, Mary S. and John F		55	38
Rodgers, Mary J	part of	53	38
Robey, John Randolph	part of	76	3
Rhode, William L		130	38
Roberts, John N	part of	2	5
Roberts, Mary M		106	36
Roberts, Lemuel	part of	169	38
Roberts Rachel C	part of	22	19
Roller, John Jacob		334	38
Roth, Martin		344	38
Rodman, Sarah E		271	38
Roberts, Edward	part of	9	39
Rollins, Thaddeus S	part of	223	32
Roche, John D	part of	158	36
Roberts, Levi P	part of	210	37
Rowley, Benjamin		174	39
Rother, Lillie	part of	201	36
Robbins, Enos R	part of	141	39
Rost, Paul		179	39

OWNERS' NAMES.	Lot No.	Section
Rogge, Ernst J	191	39
Rosebrock, Herman H...........part of	108	15
Rosebrock, Frederick W ....part of	108	15
Roesmeier, Christina Elenora	261	39
Robertson, James E.	69	29
Roth, Mary	34	36
Rouse, Mary R.	165	37
Rowley, William Henry	274	37
Rosenbaum, Christopher J., Jr.	371	37
Robinson, Benjamin A. and Margaret E	328	39
Roach, William J., John C. and Walling.......part of	337	39
Roberts, James E.	74	29
Rondthaler, J. Albert	241	39
Rhoads, Gould R ....part of	382	38
Roney, Charles S	204	36
Rocker, Margaret and John C	493	39
Robinson, Minnie May	485	39
Roberts, Margaret L.	320	37
Ross, Emma	261	37
Robinson, Mrs. Laura A ....part of	60	3
Roach, A. L.	2	1
Robson, William H., Dirce and Kate L. ....part of	409 and 410	37
Rohr, Mrs. Louisa...............part of	464	39
Royster, William L.	300	37
Ruschaupt, Henry M., Heirs of	1, 2 and 6	2
Rush, Fred P....................part of	32	8
Russell, David	52	4
Ruckle, N. R ....part of	24	12
Ruth, Charles..........part of	189	16
Ruddell, J. H. and Ambrose G.	67	13
Russell, William H.	3	19
Ruth, Robert	50	17
Rudy, Ezra H. ....part of	26	9
Ruske, Catherine	100	25
Russell, Alexander W., Heirs of	11	11
Ruskaup, Frederick	46	25
Rupp, John	226	25
Ruth, Louis G.	19	27

CROWN HILL CEMETERY. 173

OWNERS' NAMES.		Lot No.	Section
Ruddell, N. T.	part of	96	31
Rusch, Anna		286	31
Ruschhaupt, Catharine Mary		29	18
Ruschhaupt, August		30	18
Ruschhaupt, Henry C.		26	18
Rubin, Jacob		19 and 20	18
Ruckersfeldt, Mary B.		130 and 147	18
Rubusch, William G.		89	34
Russe, Conrad	part of	253	25
Rubush, George A.		173	32
Russell, Samuel and Mary		312	35
Rubush, William R. and George W.		102	33
Russell, James S.		151	35
Russe, William H		326	35
Rupert, Frank H.	part of	52	36
Ruper, Randolph	part of	52	36
Rudasel, Marila		115	38
Ruse, Thomas	part of	346	32
Ruhlmann, Eugene		19	37
Rusch, Frederick		185	34
Rusie, William A.		11	39
Ruckelshaus, Conrad		216	36
Runnells, Orange S. and Alice		50	13
Rubush, John T.	part of	268	39
Rupp, Susan		208	25
Ruckersfeldt, Tillie	part of	64	15
Rudisell, Martin L.		554	39
Ryan, Geo. W., Sr., Geo. W., Jr., Hezekiah J.		269	32
Ryder, Elizabeth		180	18
Ryan, George W		194	35
Ryan, John A.		277	35
Ryan, Anna	part of	76	38
Ryder, Joseph M	part of	40	36
Staub, I.	part of	57	5
Sanburn, Mrs. C. A		148	4
Sharp, J. K		16	3
Shaw, Elizabeth		72	4
Stark, Gustavus		160	4

OWNERS' NAMES.	Lot No.	Section
Starling, Samuel	14	2
Sharpe, Thomas H .... part of	1	12
Spann, John S	12	29
Stanton, A. P.	53	5
Swain, Mrs. Mary J	33	5
Schaub, Henry	154	4
Schaub, John	159	4
Schaub, Caroline	19	16
Small, Hattie E.	17	16
Shattuck, David J	118	16
Strassner, Mrs. Fred	122	16
Schrader, C. .... part of	42	12
Shaw, Angusta D	67	17
Salge, Frederick	39	17
Schad, Christian .... part of	33	19
Schaefer, William	49	20
Small, Elizabeth	70	20
Spratt, John E.	4	25
Swartz, Allie W.	5	31
Smart, Hezekiah	37	14
Sharpe, Andrew W	152	25
Shaw, B. C.	5	21
Spratt, Amanda J.	41	21
Sailors, J. L.	74	25
Schaub, Peter	50	25
Schnabel, John .... part of	48	25
Schad, George	48	31
Stacy, Emma J .... part of	50	14
Sharpe, William H.	45	27
Stahlhuth, Elizabeth	155	31
Sanders, Nancy J	98	25
Sandsbury, William H	73	31
Share, George K.	172	27
Salla, W. G.	122	31
Schaaf, Valentine	124	27
Shartle, E. Y .... part of	11	15
Saylor, Jackson	145	31
Scanlin, Eliza	185	31

OWNERS' NAMES.	Lot No.	Section
Sharp, Stephen ... part of	75 and 74	27
Stanley, Isaac L.	255	31
Schad, Gottlieb and Rosina M.	256	31
Shafer, Peter.	268	31
Sanders, Mary E.	262	32
Spaulding, Ralph	241	32
Schramm, J. C. A. .... part of	151	27
Schrader, Sophia .... part of	114	27
Santo, Edward.	208	32
Staton, Samuel and Sarah	13	18
Stapp, Thomas B.	152	32
Snavely, John D.	17	18
Schaub, Joseph H	73	33
Shaffer, Elizabeth	41	33
Shaw, Martha A. .... part of	4	29
Stratford, Alfred A.	260	18
Slate, Permaly A	297	18
Staubbs, James E.	73	34
Salisbury, Percival A	75	34
Scantlin, Rickey	15	34
Sapp, Mrs. Anna .... sub 1	58	20
Sapp, Jennie E. .... part of	248	25
Stark, Christian.	27	35
Shafer, Adolphus C	142	35
Sanders, John. .... part of	279	35
Schrader, August. .... part of	114	27
Schandorf, John W.	103	33
Schakel, Anton, Henry, Louisa and Mary	335	31
Shaw, Niccas E.	366	35
Starbrock, Frederick	248	35
Sanders, John	37	37
Samuels, Eva L. and Frank W ...... part of	65	35
Sanborn, Abram G.	214	35
Sharpe, Lottie.	89	37
Standiford, Joshua C. and Sarah H	100	37
Snapp, Julia.	90	35
Shawver, Emma H .... part of	253	35
Schaefer, Andrew .... part of	303	35

OWNERS' NAMES.		Lot No.	Section
Sahm, Albert	part of	233	25
Slawson, Catharine		43	38
Spaulding, Catharine	part of	121	38
Swanston, William	part of	57	14
Sawyer, Martha M	part of	36	6
Sarber, Adaline S	part of	87	20
Spahr, Franklin L		155	36
Shaw, Melville F	part of	87	36
Spacke, Mary	part of	24	19
Slate, Thomas Henry	part of	27	36
Scharn, John H. and Doris		43	36
Sanders, Henry L		131	37
Shaw, Christine		157	38
Shaw, Celia	part of	75	36
Sawyer, Edward W	part of	239	36
Sage, Mary Annie		148	37
Schaffer, Cornelius		21	3
Schandorf, Nicholas		87	5
Saltkorn, Mrs. Matilda		165	16
St. Paul's Cathedral Church		180	4
Spratt, Walter S		83	34
Sprague, Laura F		171	34
Schlake, William and Henry	part of	316	31
Schaler, Mary A	part of	165	38
Starr, Harriet		41	39
Sanders, William		11	37
Sanders, James		305	38
Slaughter, George B		206	37
Sahuk, Barbara		200	37
Spalding, James R		202	37
Stanton, Sarah		146	36
Shaneberger, Georgianna	part of	80	5
Schmalholtz, Rudolph		193	39
Staton, Furman J		202	36
Schaffer, Edward L		275	38
Schwartz, Peter H		397	39
Schmalfeldt, William		374	39
Seahill, Mrs. Maria	part of	27	17

OWNERS' NAMES.	Lot No.	Section
Schwalb, Carrie........................ part of	3	17
Shaffer, Charles A..................... part of	181	36
Swanagan, Bettie	317	37
St. Clair, William M.........................	271	39
Schrake, Henrietta S.........................	250	38
Staley, Michael C...................... part of	299	39
Sanders, Margaret............................	364	37
Sprague, Mada G.............................	290	37
Schwartze, Amalia	15	37
Sage, Stephen G........................ part of	487	39
Sparks, William A...................... part of	156	38
Sauter, Eva............................. part of	403	37
Swain, Thomas E............................	384	39
Schaub, Mrs. Ada	483	39
Schaaf, Abel........................... part of	501	39
Shawber, John	431	37
Schwartz, Elizabeth C.................. part of	352	39
Sharrard, Newton	462	37
Seaton, John L..............................	28	4
Seaman, E..................................	39	5
Stevens, Dr. Thad M.........................	31 and 32	5
Stevenson, C. S.............................	84	5
Sheets, William.............................	34 and 38	6
Smelser, James W...........................	21	2
Shellenberger, John	45	1
Scheubner, Gottlieb.........................	26	5
Sells, Michael..............................	98	2
Sterrett, Mrs. S. D..........................	37	5
Stewart, Robert M...........................	50	2
Stewart, Mrs. Sophia W......................	44 and 54	4
Seig, Mrs. George B.........................	55	4
Seger, Jonathan M...........................	24	16
Sweinheart, William	198	16
Second Presbyterian Church..................	102	16
Server, Granville............................	54	16
Steinhauer, Fred, George and Michael.........	160 and 161	16
Steeg, John L. F....................... part of	78	15
Secrest, Charles.............................	55	15

OWNERS' NAMES.	Lot No.	Section.
Scheigert, Wilhelmina	142	16
Stein, Ferdinand	52	20
Severn, Henry	25	14
Schley, Amelia M	18	20
Seiders, William H	7	13
Shea, Michael and James R	66	20
Sedgwick, Mrs. Sarah J........part of	46	19
Spehring, Frederick........part of	77	19
Seeman, Christine	31	9
Sellers, George	170	16
Selking, William	51	21
Stewart, William W., John Edward and Anna...part of	7	20
Seitz, Rosa	28	21
Shelton, Henry	87	25
Sweetser, James N........part of	24 and 25	21
Seibert, George William........part of	86 and 87	17
Sherwood, Mrs. Emma L.	167	25
Stewart, Margaret F. and Martha C........part of	18	23
Sweet, D. H.	54	27
Stern, M. G. J	53	27
Stephenson, Orville J.	52	27
Stein, John	11	27
Steidel, Susanna C........part of	180	25
Steller, Leah A........part of	129	31
Stedman, Mrs. Hannah J........part of	40	7
Stem, John........part of	75	19
Schley, John........part of	189	25
Steep, John	121	27
Schetter, Christopher	261	31
Sterrett, John F.	176	31
Steinmetz, John	28	32
Sheets, William A	247	31
Seifert, Mrs. Belle	4	32
Sebern, Nancy J	12 and 33	32
Schneider, Joseph........part of	264	32
Schmedel, Hiram	239	32
Seidensticker, Adolph........part of	36	3
Speer, Joshua K	281	31

CROWN HILL CEMETERY.

OWNERS' NAMES.	Lot No.	Section
Swhear, Herman W	59	32
Steadman, Dr. E. P., Heirs of	116	32
Steinhilber, Anna Judith	71	32
Sherman, Charles H .... part of	5	15
Scheuer, John .... part of	267	32
Searcy, J. W.	198	32
Spreng, Caroline	237	31
Shearer, Charles J. W.	138	32
Stein, Theodore	147	32
Seibert, Cicero	165	25
Sherfey, Benjamin B	139	18
Stevenson, Anna B	153	18
Steinmeyer, Christian F	168	18
Sheets, Joseph R	133	32
Schellschmidt, Adolph	46 and 57	18
Steiner, Charles	51	33
Speake, Gardner W	132	33
Steffen, Bridget	220	18
Shepard, Silas M	33	34
Sewell, Elmer C .... part of	6	7
Seidensticker, Margaret	308	32
Stewart, Andrew J .... part of	54	33
Stewart, Mrs. Maret .... part of	255	25
Stewart, Adoniram J .... part of	138	33
Stein, Thomas C	117	34
Schearrer, Christian B	143	34
Stevens, Henry C	165	34
Selb, Matthias .... part of	153	33
Stevens, Charles H	289	18
Shepherd, James McB	92, 93, 107 and 108	34
Steehan, Otto .... part of	233	25
Stevenson, Charles .... sub 14	58	20
Schelski, George H	150	35
Sellers, John	243	35
Steeg, Sarah E .... sub 2	41	20
Sheppard, Joseph H .... sub 3	41	20
Seiner, C. F.	110	35
Schreick, Charlotte .... sub 2	8	20

OWNERS' NAMES.

Owner		Lot No.	Section
Stehling, Caroline	sub 4	8	20
Spencer, Charles N		51	35
Stephenson, Mary A	part of	246	35
Spellman, Sabra V	part of	35	35
Stewart, Margaret	part of	171	35
Smelser, Phoebe	part of	2	35
Stewart, Alice	part of	2	35
Sering, Samuel		251	35
Stericher, Margaret		285	35
Scherer, Julia A		42	37
Steinbrugge, Frank and Anna		260	35
Steiner, Louis		37	38
Stewart, Thomas		80	38
Schlegel, Emanuel		345	35
Schwenk, Louis	part of	118	38
Steinruck, Joseph		112	38
Sherman, Paul	part of	40	36
Seward, George B	part of	160	38
Steele, Thomas J		150	38
Stedfeld, Henry	part of	111	27
Service, Sarah Gage		188	38
Sextroh, Henry William		18	36
Sweeney, Martha A	part of	195	38
Sherwood, William P	part of	127	37
Sherman, Emily J	part of	103	36
Steinwenter, Katharina		54	32
Shepherd, Kate C	part of	2	36
Stewart, Sarah E	part of	182	35
Shea, James H	part of	212	36
Schneider, Mary Katharina		3	39
Stewart, Harriet B		11	2
Schneider, Conrad		5	9
Schley, John, Pres., his successors in trust I. T. U		1 and 2	25
Schweinsberger, Henry		177	35
Schmertz, Minnie C	part of	394	38
Schsler, Anna E	part of	117	33
Stewart, Martha A	part of	38	29
Shelby, Arthur H		185	37

LOOKING EAST FROM WEST ENTRANCE.

CROWN HILL CEMETERY.

OWNERS' NAMES.	Lot No.	Section
Shepperd, John .... part of	119	37
Shearer, Minerva .... part of	256	36
Shearer, Samuel H. .... part of	256	36
Steinmark, Mary A.	134	39
Streett, James A. .... part of	7	36
Settle, Christiana A.	199	39
Schneider, Mary	178	39
Stearns, Henry .... part of	155	39
Stewart, Mary A.	60	29
Seekamp, Louisa R.	359	37
Shreve, Margaret L.	265	39
Svendsen, Christina	342	39
Seibert, Mary Elizabeth	112	36
Shreve, Jessie .... part of	331	37
Seibert, Ida M.	306	37
Sweet, Anna L., Elizabeth S. and Cuba H	482	39
Shea, Michael J. .... part of	86	15
Steffens, Elizabeth F.	299	37
Steele, Jennie L.	279	37
Schreckengost, Frank	334	37
Stevens, John .... part of	296	39
Sleight, William T.	430	37
Shelton, Charles S.	425	37
Sewall, Mrs. May Wright .... part of	24	13
Stephen, Joseph Z. .... part of	362	39
Scherer, Margaret	432	37
Slemmer, Mary L.	233	39
Self, David A. .... part of	311	39
Smith, Mrs. J. R.	47	1
Smith, Mrs. C. B.	9	5
Smith, Frank	14	5
Smith, Andrew	132	2
Smith, J. C. .... part of	7	1
Smith, W. Q.	134	4
Smith, Daniel R.	136	2
Smith, Mrs. Margaret	105	2
Smith, Marcus L.	137	2
Smith, Fuller	75	2

OWNERS' NAMES.	Lot No.	Section
Smith, Mrs. Ellen	27 and 28	16
Smith, Henry	375	32
Smith, James M	184	16
Smith, William	49	12
Smith, William F	163	16
Smith, Mrs. Sophia	48	17
Smith, J. E	123	4
Smith, George W .... part of	96	15
Smith, Christian	83	20
Smith, John .... part of	60	20
Smith, Mrs. Minnie	11	8
Smith, Wm. H. and George C ...... part of	60	3
Smith, John C	19	21
Smith, J. W .... part of	35	9
Smith, Sarah B	32	21
Smith, Charlie .... part of	63	21
Smith, Joseph W .... part of	95	15
Smith, Margaret .... part of	86	20
Smith, Hezekiah, Jr	58 and 59	31
Smith, Ben W .... part of	299	31
Smith, William and Emily J	238	31
Smith, Elizabeth D	210	31
Smith, Sarah C	69	32
Smith, Adoniram J	62	18
Smith, Margaret	114	33
Smith, Elizabeth A. and William J	46	33
Smith, Mrs. Maria	102	34
Smith, John	37	34
Smith, Martha Jane	146	18
Smith, Catharine M	126	18
Smith, Aaron C	303	18
Smith, James H. O	126	34
Smith, Cyrus .... part of	303	32
Smith, George M	123	33
Smith, Mary E	116	34
Smith, William H .... part of	12	14
Smith, Alfred	154	35
Smith, William F	201	35

OWNERS' NAMES.		Lot No.	Section
Smith, Anna M		235	35
Smith, Edward Athlick	part of	72	3
Smith, Frank E	part of	1	35
Smith, Henry		116	18
Smith, Catharine		269	35
Smith, George C		9	38
Smith, Leroy B		50	38
Smith, Walter S	part of	12	38
Smith, Catharine	part of	16	27
Smith, Henry C		185	38
Smith, Hattie J		20	37
Smith, Fountain P	part of	4	20
Smith, Bridget J		187	38
Smith, Oskaloosa M		193	38
Smith, William J		17	37
Smith, John C	part of	137	33
Smith, Eliza		352	38
Smith, Mary A	part of	26	27
Smith, August C		84	33
Smith, Sarah	part of	150	37
Smith, John J		104	36
Schmidt, C. F		2	8
Schmidt, F	part of	103	2
Schmidt, Lorenz		103	15
Schmidt, Mrs. Elizabeth		51	16
Schmid, Johanna C		29	20
Schmidt, Charles J		38	19
Schmitt, George		64	25
Schmidt, August		99	16
Schmidt, J. Henry		126	31
Schmidt, Peter		94 and 95	31
Schmidt, Clara		82	31
Schmidt, Robert		197	32
Schmidt, William A		64	33
Schmidt, Magdalena		172	35
Schmidt, William		181	38
Smith, Elias P	part of	74	37
Schmidt, Fredericka		209	38

OWNERS' NAMES.	Lot No.	Section
Smith, Marion F.	246	37
Smith, Barbara	196	37
Smith, William C .... part of	53	15
Smith, Jesse .... part of	75	21
Schmidt, Henry and Lillie D	420	39
Smith, Samuel W .... part of	164	38
Smith, Theodore L .... part of	399	39
Smith, Henry M. and James B	216	39
Smith, Sarah M	288	37
Smith, Catherine .... part of	15	38
Schmidt, Christina	332	37
Schmidt, Christian .... part of	233	25
Smith, Mrs. Nancy	484	39
Smith, Wirt C. and Jeannette	253	38
Smith, Mrs. Jennie	372	37
Skillen, James and William	21	6
Simpson, Valentine and Elizabeth, Heirs of	77, 78 and 79	5
Sinker, Edward T.	16	6
Swift, Henry J .... part of	201	16
Swift, Lydia E .... part of	167 and 168	16
Stiltz, J. George .... part of	13	3
Springer, John M.	8	19
Springsteen, Abraham S., Sr. and Abraham F. S.	67	14
Spiegel, Augustus	40	15
Snider, L .... part of	27	15
Stringer, W. H .... part of	54	20
Schindler, Mrs. S. V.	71	21
Siler, Mrs. Sophia	27	21
Schierling, Herman .... part of	90	17
Schickentanz, Jacob .... part of	74	16
Sinclair, Mrs. Elizabeth L	48	14
Shipp, Joseph P .... part of	21	23
Smither, John, James W. and Henry C .... part of	236	25
Smither, Theodore F., Robert G. and John W ... part of	236	25
Sinclair, Mary T.	196	31
Springer, Elizabeth Jane	100	31
Swindler, Benjamin F. and Anna D	189	31
Snider, James A. W	305	31

CROWN HILL CEMETERY.

OWNERS' NAMES.	Lot No.	Section
Snider, David W..	306	31
Snider, Mary E .. part of	193	25
Sipe, A. K........	269	31
Spielhoff, Henry .... part of	117	27
Stirk, David P........	253	32
Schilling, Henry	237	32
Shirk, Samuel S........	121 and 122	32
Springer, David, Heirs of..	290	31
Simpson, Charles A......... part of	202	25
Schwinge, Louisa F.........	228	32
Sindlinger, Peter.. part of	46	15
Shipp, Samuel M ...... part of	337	31
Schwinge, August H. .... part of	53	22
Shilling, Mrs. Alice C .... part of	135	32
Shilling, Mrs. Merab T........ part of	135	32
Sickels, Christina	86	18
Silvers, Walter B .... part of	255	25
Schildmeier, Charles C. and Katie........	287	32
Sickel, Ferdinand .... part of	72	18
Strickland, Joseph....... part of	24	34
Steinecker, Harmon H........	48	34
Simon, Louis .... part of	118	33
Shilling, Monroe	294	18
Sinclair, Sarah J........	122	34
Simmons, Benjamin F. and Harry........	29	34
Schissel, Otto........	105	34
Shimer, Corydon R........ part of	53	22
Springer, Daniel M	65	34
Shillinger, Barbara........	309	18
Shields, Priscilla .... sub 10	25	20
Stirk, Tillie........ sub 5	58	20
Simon, Eva........ part of	113	33
Sickler, Isaac H........ part of	127 and 131	27
Shingleton, Annie........ part of	305	35
Shingleton, Henry........	222	35
Swift, Elias B........	45	35
Shingleton, Ronald Thomas........ part of	223	35
Sirp, William........ part of	164	35

CROWN HILL CEMETERY

OWNERS' NAMES.		Lot No.	Section
Shideler, Charlotte M.	part of	67	35
Shimer, William R.	part of	34	22
Simco, William (Administrator).		10	37
Schmidlap, Lewis		355	35
Simpson, Elizabeth D		40	35
Sieboldt, Anna	part of	16	38
Springer, George W		24	38
Spitzfaden, Peter		70	36
Springer, Martin B.		2	38
Stillinger, Fannie	part of	121	38
Spiegel, Christian		11	38
Stickney, Ida M		54	36
Sickler, Edward E.	part of	127	27
Stillwell, Harry Herbert	part of	87	20
Simpson, Lucetta		21	37
Schimmel, Charles.		173	36
Simpson, Margaret A	part of	25	1
Simpson, Alfred B.		385	38
Stiles, Amanda	part of	353	38
Smitherman, Julius J.		56	37
Stier, Christian.	part of	133	35
Simpson, William B.	part of	345	38
Simpson, Maria Janet	part of	345	38
Singleton, Henry		28	37
Sinker, Herman	part of	179	38
Scrimsher, Joseph W. and Charles F		31	39
Stinecker, Ernest	part of	24	17
Stiarwalt, Van Buren.		43	31
Simmerlink, John and F		117	31
Simmons, Annie E.		308	18
Swisher, William F.		225	39
Spilman, Oliver P.	part of	87	31
Scrimger, Ura.		209	39
Stilt, Emma P.		199	37
Snider, George W		109	36
Simonsen, Minnie	part of	341	39
Shields, Eva	part of	124	39
Skinner, Bessie F		72	39

Owners' Names		Lot No.	Section
Schierling, Charles H.	part of	90	17
Smithson, Grant		381	37
Shilling, William E		82	39
Simmons, Nellie P.	part of	470	39
Schindler, Margaret		147	36
Stone, William O.		23	1
Sloan, George W		11	6
Stokes, Richard M.	part of	37	7
Schooley, Thomas	part of	6	8
Scott, Adam		142	2
Shoemaker, Amanda	part of	25	16
Sohl, Levi		67	3
Stowell, Myra A	part of	60	16
Schofield, Nathan M		37	12
Southard, James W		149	16
Soper, S. R.		114	16
Schwomeyer, Charles	part of	84	16
Shoeneman, William	part of	83	16
Strong, Samuel P		62	19
Shoup, Calvin T.	part of	17	19
Stoelting, Magdalena		4	19
Scott, William		100	16
Sproule, Mrs. Mary F		17	20
Smock, R. M		19	15
Stormer, P. E		34 and 35	20
Showalter, S.		93	17
Sommar, August	part of	42	15
Scott, Frank N		164	37
Stofer, John	part of	16	21
Soehner, Charles	part of	60	13
Schroder, Rachel	part of	79	19
Stout, Mrs. Elizabeth		26	13
Sponable, Mary Jane		154	25
Strowe, Emily	part of	62	25
Smock, Peter D		172	25
Show, William		48	27
Scofield, Mrs. Emeline	part of	73	3
Stout, Mrs. Catherine		45 and 46	31

CROWN HILL CEMETERY.

OWNERS' NAMES.	Lot No.	Section
Stout, W. F.	152	31
Scott, Samuel, D.	57	25
Schofield, David B.	69	19
Souers, Andrew	72	31
Shortridge, A. C.	74	15
Sobbe, Charles .... part of	179	25
Scott, John	146	31
Stroupe, Peter .... part of	3	3
Schoettle, Christian	66	27
Schroerlucke, Johanna	182	31
Schroer, Herman H	278	31
Soliday, Mrs. Flora .... part of	220	25
Scott, A. A. .... part of	77	27
Schowe, William F	256	32
Schowe, Frederick	243	32
Schloer, Christian .... part of	209	25
Stone, D. E. .... part of	31	3
Schoppenhorst, W., Heirs of ...... part of	14	23
Stolte, William .... part of	266	32
Schowe, George F.	57	32
Schlotzhauer, Adam	252	31
Schoeneman, Charles .... part of	333	32
Stockman, George W.	312	32
Shoemaker, John C.	3	29
Scott, John E. .... part of	3	15
Schlotzhauer, Valentine .... part of	256	25
Stout, Furman and George W.	2	14
South, James M.	149	33
Strong, William	15	33
Schoen, George	80	34
Schonacker, Belle C.	186	34
Smock, Louisa	154	18
Spotts, William .... part of	254	25
Sonnefield, William	144	34
Shook, Elias	147	34
Stover, Daniel	109	34
Schooley, David	121	34
Smock, William C.	198	34

OWNERS' NAMES.		Lot No.	Section
Schroeder, Ferdinand	part of	21	19
Spong, Thomas E		105	35
Sommer, Margaretta	sub 4	72	20
Sponsel, Henry		144	35
Sowders, Mary Elizabeth		8	37
Shoemaker, Charles J	part of	167	35
Short, Clara	part of	84	27
Stroble, John	part of	2	12
Sommerlad, Christopher		353	32
Stokes, Jacob C	part of	254	35
Smock, Howard	part of	332	31
Shonesy, Jane		39	38
Short, Willard N	part of	367	32
Sockwell, Henry M	part of	238	25
South, John and Albert		41	36
Schoeneman, John W	part of	179	38
Soult, Jane		95	37
Stoops, Catherine E., Mary and Ellsworth		87	37
Stokely, Sarah	part of	121	37
Schroerlucke, John	part of	52	39
Scott, Martha A	part of	38	29
Sloan, Frances M		155	37
Sommer, Louis		46	39
Schofield, William		186	37
South, Teressa E	part of	195	38
Scott, Daniel L	part of	210	38
Stockwell, Palmer R	part of	210	38
Stout, Alice M		118	39
Stossmeister, Fred		165	39
Strobel, George J. and William R	part of	131	39
Stockton, Washington W	part of	47	38
Scott, William P	part of	372	39
Shoemaker, Henry F	part of	200	36
Scott, John		243	39
Sloan, Harry M		447	39
Schoershusen, Christian H	part of	114	39
Shortridge, Ambrose F	part of	267	38
Smoot, Lucy and Edward J	part of	334	39

CROWN HILL CEMETERY.

OWNERS' NAMES.		Lot No.	Section
Schooley, Benjamin F	part of	362	37
Slough, Nettie M		363	39
Stocker, Isaac		313	37
Schroeder, Gustave I	part of	440	39
Sponsel, Henry G		463	39
Shover, James E. and Emma F	part of	83	14
Short, Cora L		267	37
Somerville, Thomas M. and Theodore E		442	39
Schoen, Henry and John		461	39
Somerville, James		136	36
Sullivan, William, Sr		48	1
Schnull, A. and H		35	6
Sulgrove, James	part of	45	3
Sulgrove, James W	part of	45	3
Sulgrove, Milton N	part of	45	3
Suhre, John H		5	2
Stumph, John B		33	7
Summers, Caroline		74	4
Stuck, J. W		95	4
Schurman, Emma, Edward and Henry		12	13
Sutter, Mrs. Amelia		181	16
Scudder, M. R		12	19
Schultz, Henry	part of	97	15
Suhr, Frederick	part of	90	15
Sulgrove, Henry J	part of	8	21
Stumph, Joseph		137	25
Schurr, Leonard, Jr		45	21
Stuck, Peter		99	25
Sulgrove, George W	part of	23	16
Schulte, Herman	part of	129	25
Stumph, Christina		177	25
Sutton, Joseph M	part of	227	25
Scudder, Mary L. E		187	25
Summers, Katie		33	31
Summers, Sarah		109	31
Sullivan, George F		120	31
Schumacher, John A		88	31
Summers, William		259	31

OWNERS' NAMES.	Lot No.	Section
Scudder, Mrs. Jane..... part of	341	31
Stuckmeyer, Charles H................	175	27
Sutherland, W. H....................	1	18
Schulmeyer, Louis............ part of	314	31
Sutter, Caroline.....................	79	18
Shuler, Lawrence S..................	322 and 323	32
Shutt, Jacob F......................	316	32
Sullivan, William............. part of	130	27
Schuler, Frank	246	18
Suesz, Charles......................	167	33
Shulse, John M. C .... part of	169	34
Spurrier, Francis H..................	312	18
Suhr, Henry William.................	164	33
Scudder, Lillie M .... sub 3	25	20
Stultz, John W .... sub 1	82	17
Sturm, Henry H.....................	6	35
Shufelton, Thomas P.......... part of	119	35
Suhr, Mary.........................	44	37
Stuck, Robert.......................	237	35
Sullivan, Mrs. Louisa................	84	37
Stumph, Elizabeth...................	100	33
Schuck, Louis .... part of	3	20
Scudder, Mattie.....................	76	37
Stumph, George W..................	107	33
Schumacher, Henry A. and Barbara...	85	33
Suhr, Henry F......................	17	39
Sullivan Dennis.....................	306	38
Stuckey, Charles............. part of	262	36
Stumph, Lulu................ part of	33	35
Schumacher, John A.................	197	36
Schuck, Minnie.....................	200	39
Shufelton, Margaret A	106	39
Sutton, Sarah J	260	39
Schubert, George W.................	267	39
Schultz, August.....................	292	38
Sulgrove, Anna Laura......... part of	301	39
Schultz, Mary L.....................	412	37
Suffren, Mrs. Louisa J	4	16

CROWN HILL CEMETERY.

OWNERS' NAMES.   Lot No.   Section

Owner		Lot No.	Section
Sutherland, David J. and James W.		432	39
Snyder, Amanda J.		6	18
Snyder, George W.		207	18
Sym, Mrs. Jane	part of	138	33
Snyder, John J	part of	130	33
Styer, Martin R.		264	18
Sylvester, Jane W.		125	34
Syters, Rufus K.	part of	2	6
Snyder, Henrietta		319	35
Symons, Samantha		361	38
Snyder, Luella	part of	22	21
Snyder, Fred M	part of	167	35
Taylor, William H.		153	4
Tapking, F. H.		57	5
Taggart, Samuel		40	3
Talbot, Richard L.	part of	19	1
Tapking, John F.		58	5
Thayer, George		22	1
Talbott, W. H.		3	8
Talbott, John M		10	8
Taylor, John		59	4
Taylor, Napoleon B.		10	1
Thayer, Selden	part of	75	4
Thrasher, William M.		18	12
Talbott, Charles H.		13	12
Traub, Israel		111	16
Traub, Jacob J		126	16
Traub, Charles		127	16
Tarkington, W. C.		111	14
Traub, Jacob		110	16
Taylor, Samuel		62	20
Talbot, Henry	part of	34	17
Taggart, John A.		53	25
Thalman, Elizabeth		41	25
Taylor, Jane B.		4	27
Taylor, William C	part of	16	27
Tallentire, Thomas and William G.		156	32
Trask, Abby	part of	147	25

OWNERS' NAMES.		Lot No.	Section
Talbot, Joseph C., Bishop of Indiana..	part of	19	1
Travis, Albert..................	part of	150	32
Tramer, Conrad.................		213	31
Taylor, Joseph M................		8	18
Tarlton, James A................	part of	319	31
Talbert, Margaret C..............		99	18
Thalman, Isaac..................	part of	191	27
Taylor, Isaac, Irwin and Edgar L.....		309	32
Taylor, Violena C................	part of	173	34
Tanner, Mary...................	sub 8	92	20
Taylor, George O................		308	35
Taylor, David M. and Jesse........	part of	69	4
Thaught, Charles................		140	35
Trayford, George................		83	37
Talge, John B...................		75	35
Thaeter, John A.................	part of	103	38
Tatman, Frank T................		343	35
Taylor, William G...............		341	35
Taggart, Patterson F.............		183	37
Taylor, Clara A.................	part of	110	15
Traub, Charles G................	part of	131	39
Taggart, Joseph.................	part of	82	21
Tamblyn, John F. and Henry W.....		166	37
Taylor, Major...................		233	36
Thayer, Martha A...............	part of	31	21
Traub, Gottloeb E. C.............	part of	381	39
Taylor, Phoebe M., William M. and Mary Lewis......		59	14
Thatcher, James H...............	part of	121	36
Test, Charles S..................		120	16
Teine, Christian.................	part of	75	19
Teckinbrock, H. W...............	part of	158	25
Teckinbrock, Christian...........	part of	158	25
Teneyck, John...................		77	31
Treitschke, William..............		108	31
Teneycke, Mary A...............		67	31
Teepe, Dina.....................		123	27
Temple, Hannah B...............	part of	248	32
Trester, David..................		284	31

OWNERS' NAMES.	Lot No.	Section
Terry, W. R.	229	32
Teague, Rebecca P.	74	33
Teague, Franklin	75	33
Techentin, Henry............. part of	93	33
Terrell, George F.	80	18
Trenary, John W.	44	34
Telfer, Mrs. Louisa	203	34
Trenary, Julia M.	177	34
Templeton, Aaron D............ part of	173	34
Tercy, John	85	34
Tevis, Virgil W. and Mary P.	191	32
Tevis, John S.	11	34
Tweed, Charles E	353	35
Teufel, Flora................ part of	394	38
Teckenbrock, Rebecca......... part of	169	37
Telkamp, Catherine Mary...... part of	103	38
Tellkamp, Catherine Mary	320	39
Tetaz, Harry L............... part of	30	27
Tilford, J. M	44	3
Tinsley, William	43	7
Trindle, Samuel	89	20
Tilt, Rebecca A	25	25
Trindle, John................. part of	91	20
Tinder, H. M.	109	32
Thiesing, Joseph	206	18
Tieter, Ernest................ part of	72	18
Tindall, Gertrude............. part of	332	38
Timmerman, Herman	54	39
Tilford, John C.............. part of	288	38
Twiname, James E.	293	37
Timmerman, Herman H	306	39
Tripp, Enoch W	357	37
Tilton, Cyrineus H	182	36
Tielking, Henry W.	386	39
Todhunter E.	100	2
Tonsey, Oliver	1	5
Tout, Wilkinson M.	48	4
Tomlinson, James M	40, 41, 42 and 43	2

WINTER SCENE.

CROWN HILL CEMETERY.

OWNERS' NAMES.	Lot No.	Section
Tousey, George	9	8
Tout, Nancy	50	4
Thompson, Henry .... part of	150	4
Thomas, Robert	80	4
Thomas, John	52	7
Thorne, John	84	2
Thoms, Frederick	52	3
Tout, Isaac W	20	16
Thomas, George, Sr	200	16
Thompson, Q .... part of	104	2
Thompkins, J. H. F.	108	16
Thompson, Eli	78	17
Thom, John, William and Charles ..... part of	6	20
Thompson, John F	21	9
Thomas, Wm. G .... part of	16	9
Thomas, Louis L.	103	25
Thompson, W. A	47	25
Tout, Mary A	2	31
Trotter, Mrs. Amanda Jane	56	31
Todd, Henry P	298	31
Thompson, Alfred	207	31
Thoms, Thomas	39	32
Trost, John	51	32
Thompson, W. A. and Mrs. H	95	32
Thompson, George H .... part of	6	7
Thomas, Ephraim	192	32
Toole, Peter M	142	32
Tout, Asa C	33	18
Topp, Charles .... part of	318	31
Thoms, Mrs. Ella	22	33
Trou, William	101	34
Thompson, Henry H	268	18
Thompson, Mary A .... part of	21	23
Thornton, Daniel T .... part of	129	27
Thompson, Edward P .... part of	22	8
Thompson, Julia A	154	34
Thomas, Seth E .... sub 2	1	17
Thomas, Nettie .... sub 2	85	17

OWNERS' NAMES.	Lot No.	Section
Thomson, Hugh, Estate of............ sub 1	72	20
Thom, John	67	20
Thompson, Thomas and Ella............	323	35
Tool, Emma A........................ part of	178	4
Thomson, Lydia...................... part of	29	4
Thomson, Alexander.................. part of	8	6
Thompson, Charles C. and Caroline A....	51	38
Thompson, James M. and Ann E........	71	38
Thompson, Eliza.....................	72	37
Thompson, Dr. James L...............	61	37
Thompson, Charles G.................	69	37
Thompson, Richard W................ part of	170	38
Thomas, Mary A.....................	80	36
Thomas, Nathaniel F................. part of	382	38
Tolly, William V..................... part of	253	31
Topp, Frederick.....................	98	36
Thompson, Mary E...................	64	37
Thompson, Mary F...................	111	37
Thomas, Ada C......................	226	36
Throm, Katie....................... part of	207	39
Topping, George W..................	180	39
Troutwine, Martha A.................	89	39
Thompson, J. Livingston..............	5	36
Tolle, Frederick William..............	294	37
Thompson, Gideon B.................	486	39
Thomson, Henry R................... part of	121	36
Tomamichel, Joseph .... part of	403	37
Thomas, Nancy......................	461	37
Turner, James	17	3
Tuttle, Orin	89	2
Turbyville, Robert...................	116	4
Tuttle, B. F. and G. P................ part of	33	8
Tutewiler, Henry....................	26	7
Tucker, D. H.......................	77	4
Tucker, Mrs. Addie..................	175	16
Tucker, W. H. and George C.......... part of	34	19
Turner, Joanna..................... part of	62	25
Turpie, David......................	164	25

OWNERS' NAMES.	Lot No.	Section
Turner, Mrs. Starlen	14	32
Turner, Otis Willard	89	32
Turner, Henry C	151	32
Tuttle, Mary A	29	23
Trueman, Mattie A..................sub 2	92	20
Trueman, Maria T..................sub 5	92	20
Thurston, Jennie....................part of	25	3
Thurston, Ellen M...................part of	25	3
Thrush, Harry J	157	33
Trueblood, James....................part of	69	4
Tucker, Sarah H	118	35
Trueblood, Hezekiah L	217	38
Turnham, Abraham L.................part of	49	37
Tulley, Edward M...................part of	177	27
Turner, Marcus.....................part of	356	39
Tyer, George W	64	19
Tyler, Spofford E...................part of	3	13
Uphaus, Mary Ann	2	34
Uhl, John C	77	17
Underhill, Mrs. A. C.	12	5
United States Government	All of	10
Uverzayt, Herman H	19	17
Unversaw, Elizabeth	68	31
Unversaw, John N	63	33
Umphrey, Louis.....................part of	153	33
Unversaw, Andrew	215	39
Ulrey, David J.....................part of	227	39
Union Trust Co., Indianapolis, Trustees of Heirs of John Layman	315	37
Union Trust Co., Indianapolis, Trustees of Heirs of Phillip Innes	340	37
Urmston, Sarah	238	39
Van Lanningham, L	38	5
Vajen, J. H	65	1
Vail, Sidney J	133	10
Vandyke, Isaac N....................part of	65	20
Vance, Elizabeth C	143	25
Van Blaricum, Mary M	45	25

OWNERS' NAMES.	Lot No.	Section
Van Densen, Mrs. Kate............................	71	31
Vanscyoc, John W.......................... part of	243	31
Van Horn, Nicholas .... part of	267	31
Van Blaricum Newton..............................	61	32
Van Deren, Lena...................................	216	32
Van Antwerp, G. W...............................	75	32
Van Doren, Matilda A .... part of	50	3
Van Bergen, W. H..................................	278	32
Vance, Herman E........................... part of	50	3
Van Deman, Joshua H............................	108	27
Van Tuyl, Amelia...................................	95	34
Vandegrift, Martha E...................... part of	13	3
Van Pelt, Edward M........................ part of	111	33
Van Camp, Courtland.............................	16	29
Van Dyne, Eugene....................part of sub 4	81	17
Vandersaar, Wendel...............................	190	35
Van Buren, Harriet A.............................	78	36
Vanlaningham, Pearl T...........................	199	38
Vance, Thomas......................................	26	39
Van Tress, Benjamin F...........................	375	39
Vannote, Hannah...................................	226	37
Van Eaton, Charlie L...................... part of	167	36
Van Vorhis, Isaac N. and Sarah C.............	18	22
Van Osdol, Mary Francis Goodwin........ part of	78	14
Vehling, Frederick	95 and 122	18
Vehling, Henry W. C..............................	197	38
Vestal, Ada...	281	39
Vinnedge, J. D. and J. A................. part of	56 and 42	1
Vincent, William H................................	144	2
Vinton, Mrs. Theresa C..........................	66	13
Vielhaber, Daniel...................................	301	31
Vicker, Frederick	140	18
Viol, Anna K..	20	33
Vincent, Ann..	107	37
Vincent, Anna Laura..............................	123	37
Victor, Julius A............................ part of	270	38
Vinnedge, Jennie L........................ part of	301	39
Vinson, John L............................. part of	301	39

CROWN HILL CEMETERY.

OWNERS' NAMES.		Lot No.	Section
Vinnedge, Charles A.	part of	301	39
Voorhees, Jacob		142 and 143	4
Vonnegut, Clemens		52	2
Voegtle, Jacob		51	2
Voorhees, Mary J	part of	175	4
Voss, Gustavus H		5	8
Vogel, Henry		89	25
Vogt, Fred J		167	31
Vollmer, Daniel G	part of	253	31
Von Jalgerhuis, Lee		107	18
Vondergotten, Henry		113	18
Von Spreckelson, Rebecca S		129	33
Vogt, Mary	part of	110	32
Voigt, Christiana		219	35
Vogt, Henry W		89	36
Vollrath, Herman		208	39
Vogel, Carl Frederick		326	39
Wallace, Samuel		25	2
Ward, William		30	4
Wallace, William		17	6
Walker, Jacob S		57	1
Warriner, Marcus		112	2
Walpole, Miss Susan B		18	7
Wallace, Andrew W		37	6
Wallace, George C	part of	62	3
Watson, S. W	part of	12	12
Washington, Henry		121	4
Wasson, W. G		131	16
Walker, Joseph B		44	14
Wallace, William, James, Andrew and Johnston		41	15
Waugh, Daniel	part of	60	20
Walk, Mrs. Emma and Julius C		67	15
Warner, Thomas D		25	9
Wachs, Helene		57	19
Wagner, Mrs. Jennie	part of	15	21
Wands, Alexander		30	25
Wachstetter, Jacob		75	16
Wallick, John F		65	14

OWNERS' NAMES.		Lot No.	Section
Warman, Enoch and Phoebe J.	part of	32	23
Walter, Charles G. and Frances A.	part of	92	25
Wands, William and Christian	part of	151	25
Watson, Sarah J.	part of	2	4
Walpole, Esther	part of	22	13
Walden, Elias		22 and 115	27
Warren, George S.		70	27
Waterman, Dr. L. D.	part of	4	3
Washburn, Calvin		203	31
Wainwright, William H.	part of	59	27
Watts, B. F.		172	31
Watt, William H.	part of	293	31
Walton, Luvina		259	32
Wharton, Rev. Joseph W., Heirs of		116	27
Wachstetter, Charles		34	32
Ward, James E.		115	32
Waters, Annie L.		218	32
Walker, Ellen		225	31
Waite, Volney B.	part of	44	7
Wands, William R.		152	18
Ward, Boswell	part of	239	25
Walker, Anna L.	part of	31	13
Wall, David	part of	171	32
Wallingford, Charles A.		61	33
Wasson, Hiram P.		94	14
Wall, Thomas		299	18
Watts, Aaron H.		238	18
Walter, John E.		91	33
Wall, George		41	34
Watts, James E.	part of	162 and 175	18
Watson, Charles C.		99	33
Wade, Ohio L.		168	34
Way, Sarah T.	part of	374	32
Warner, Huldah V.	part of	135	33
Walters, Mary G.		170	34
Warweg, Henry and Christian		358	32
Wales, Samuel W. and Ruama W.	sub 6	1	17
Ward, Hattie E.	part of	240	25

CROWN HILL CEMETERY.

OWNERS' NAMES.

	Lot No.	Section
Wadsworth, William F., Cornelius B., Robert D. and Frank V.	70	34
Wasson, Dessa B. .... part of	155	27
Walker, Charles M .... sub 5	8	20
Wasson, Lewis	42	35
Wagner, Otto R	204	35
Wacker, August and John	333	31
Wade, Frank P	11	35
Wands, James W .... part of	150	27
Wagoner, William H	35	38
Walden, Addie	44	38
Wachstetter, Sarah Ann	295	35
Ward, Anna M .... part of	66	38
Wallace, General Lewis	3	36
Ward, Mary E .... part of	2	36
Warburton, Charles S	33	36
Warren, Edith R .... part of	340	38
Walker, Hannah .... part of	99	36
Wallmann, Dine	291	38
Wachstetter, Anna	134	36
Watts, John E .... part of	47	39
Wamsley, Charles	148	39
Wagner, Anna	158	39
Wall, Frances E.	330	37
Watkins, Mary L.	273	37
Ward, Cary J	258	37
Walker, William A .... part of	87	33
Wasson, William G.	581	39
Waterman, Frederick	454	39
Watson, John .... part of	248	39
Ward, Frederick .... part of	381	39
Waugh, Mattie W	347	37
Walker, Abraham	263	37
Walter, John	459	39
Wallace, Kate A	504	39
West, George H	15	8
West, Henry F .... part of	6	6
Wentz, W. W.	25	5

OWNERS' NAMES.	Lot No.	Section
Weaver, William W.	39	1
Wheatley, W. H. .... part of	11	1
Webster, George C. .... part of	2	3
Webb, Willis S.	8	12
Weghorst, Henry	92	2
Weigand, Anthony .... part of	7	3
Wesby, Charles E. and Ephraim	134	16
Wert, Rebecca A	10	13
Whele, Lucas	112	16
Weir, George W.	50	16
Weegman, C. H.	141	16
Webb, Joshua and Isaiah	35	17
Weber, Frederick .... part of	33	19
Wehn, Christian	79	20
Wells, Margaret	94	17
Weiland, William C. .... part of	90	15
Weaver, George	28	9
Westphal, Henry	28	25
Weikert, John	8	27
West, William C.	109	25
Weaver, Louisa E.	64	27
Weber, Jacob Frederick	115	31
Wheatley, Sarah C.	35	31
Weelburg, Maggie	125	27
Wells, Andrew J .... part of	236	25
Weiss, Annie	168	31
Weber, Susan	57	31
Weilacher, John	183	31
Wells, James H.	98	31
Welch, David	42	32
Weeks, William H.	126	32
Weirick, Drucilla	56	32
Wenning, Richard	335	32
Wheat, James C.	293	32
Welch, Amanda C.	181	32
Wheeler, William Vinson .... part of	179	27
Werbe, Fredericka	31	33
Webster, George S.	318	32

OWNERS' NAMES.	Lot No.	Section
Weeks, George............................	35	18
Weis, Anna M...................... part of	117	31
Wempner, Henry, Jr	49	33
Wheeler, William J......................	377	32
Westerfeld, William.....................	161	34
Weinberger, Herman....................	36	33
Weiland, Fred, Jr	197	34
Weaver, John H.........................	6	34
Wesbey, Medora........................	127	34
West, John R...........................	58	34
Wesp, Henry H.........................	62	34
Weber, August..........................	269	18
Weathermax, Rev. Franklin W............	174	34
Wells, Edmund......................sub 16	58	20
Wells, Alexander E................ part of	105	27
Wren, George B......................sub 10	58	20
Whetsel, Henry M.......................	141	33
Webb, Leonidas E................. part of	103	27
Wentz, Elizabeth .... part of	78	15
Weiland, William, Eli H. and Charles E....... part of	31	35
Wensley, Joseph L. and James L..........	146	35
Werther, William .... part of	8	35
Wetsell, Mary S.........................	350	35
Wehrley, Charles.......................	74	35
Wheatley, Joseph W....................	209	35
Wheeler, Elizabeth.....................	36	37
Wenz, Deborah Ann............... part of	182	35
Wetzel, Fredericka .... part of	41	38
Webb, Arthur H.........................	61	38
Weinbrecht, John G....................	101	38
Wehling, Pauline C	142	38
Wells, William F., Jr	178	38
Weaver, George R................. part of	379	38
Wheeler, Edward.................. part of	386	38
Wesling, Henry.................... part of	346	38
Wease, William H.......................	21	36
Weghorst, Marie .... part of	343	38
Weisbrod, Peter........................	323	38

CROWN HILL CEMETERY.

OWNERS' NAMES.		Lot No.	Section
Weaver, Charles M.		316	38
Whelan, Rose		3	37
Weghorst, William		23	2
Wheeler, Elizabeth		172	37
Wedewen, Evert	part of	5	39
Wesp, John and Mary A		296	38
Werner, Christian	part of	300	38
Weber, Frank L		213	39
Webster, Joseph H		395	39
Wells, Frank		306	18
Webb, Edward L	part of	266	18
Wells, Mollie	part of	8	39
Wells, Charles W	part of	87	33
Webb, Charles A		444	39
Webb, Elizabeth		88	17
Weikert, Eva	part of	65	39
Weaver, Nancy A		71	39
Weghorst, Henry H		491	39
Webb, Sewall R	part of	408	37
Weber, Louis		245	37
Weber, Peter		370	37
Williamson, M. D		24	1
Williams, Charles		30	1
Wright, William H		15	2
Wiley, William Y	part of	51	5
Wright, John C	part of	51	5
Wilson, Jonathan	part of	29 and 69	4
Willard, A. G		29	5
Williams, Jefferson	part of	73	5
Wilson, William	part of	46	2
Wilkinson, Rufus H	part of	46	2
Wright, A. L	part of	46	2
White, F. G		94	4
Willson, Charles G		30	2
Winslow, Alonzo B		38	4
Whitney, Charles C		113	2
Wiles, D. H		54	5
Wilkins, Peter		32	4

OWNERS' NAMES.	Lot No.	Section
Wright, Isaac H.	26	8
Wilson, Michael W	74	3
Witt, B. F.	20	3
Wirt, John B.	29	16
Wilcox, John C .... part of	183	16
Wright, Hiram N	116	16
Wright, Richard A	177	16
Wittinger, Jacob.	84	15
Whitman, Mrs. Anna	151	16
Wiseman, Mrs. Barbara A.	41	14
Wright, Levi	45	12
Whitehead, William	164	16
Winkle, Samuel.	36	16
Wilson, Henry C	91	14
Willcox, Charles.	64	17
Wright, Hiram.	54	17
Winter, Mrs. Mary D.	18	19
Wingate, Robert M .... part of	11	13
Wiendram, W. .... part of	90	16
White, George H. .... part of	101	16
Wilkinson, John.	53	20
Wickliff, Peter.	76	20
Wright, Theodore F	11	21
Wilson, James G.	12	9
Whitten, Mrs. Lucinda.	193	16
Whitted, John.	34	25
Wiley, James .... part of	24	13
Wiley, Mary.	7	25
Wiese, Henry .... part of	13	21
Wilson, Isaac.	13	25
White, Mary	57	21
Witman, H. N.	39	25
Wiggs, Wheeler and Elizabeth	71	25
Whitsit, Martha L. .... part of	7	21
Windsheimer, John F. .... part of	95	16
Williams, William L.	23	25
Wilson, George .... part of	66	19
Whippey, F. C. and sisters.	80	25

CROWN HILL CEMETERY.

OWNERS' NAMES.		Lot No.	Section
Witzeman, Eliza J.	part of	74	20
Wilhelm, Charles	part of	87	27
White, George W.		71	27
Williams, Daniel		39	27
Wright, Oliver		150	31
Winn, W. O.		82	27
Whiteman, John H.		37	31
Williams, Anna M., Heirs of	part of	5	3
Wilkins, John A.	part of	5	3
Williams, Henry C.		65	31
Whitney, Sarah		3	27
Willard, William		246	25
Williams, Mrs. Catharine	part of	169	31
Wiles, Mrs. Josephine	part of	244	25
White, Samuel J.	part of	210	25
Wilson, Mrs. Mary R.		241	25
Wishmire, Anthony and George	part of	185	25
Williams, Annie M. and John W.		198	25
Whitesell, William H.		21	32
Whitesell, Jacob	part of	178	32
Whitesell, John M.	part of	25	32
Wilson, John		31	32
Wilson, Mrs. Emma		227	32
Wigginton, David T.		275	32
White, Alonzo M. and Warren H.		224	31
Witthoft, Henry, Sr.		226	32
Willits, Josiah C.		39	18
Winter, Ferdinand	part of	65	13
Wilmot, Caroline A.		16	18
White, Harriet B.	part of	333	32
Winters, P. C.		75	18
Whitton, Beaumont S.		115	18
Winchester, Wilber F.	part of	320	31
Wightman, Mrs. Susie T.	part of	319	31
Wiley, George M.		58	33
Winnings, Harriet		43	33
Wilson, John T.	part of	119	33
Willard, Mrs. Frances S.		76	33

OWNERS' NAMES.	Lot No.	Section
Williamson, Joseph H	94	18
Wingate, Edwin H	241 and 245	18
Winnings, Jesse R	123	18
Wilcox, William W	50	33
Wilson, Mary M	35	34
Wright, Mrs. Nancy	173	18
White, Susan A .... part of	193	25
Williams, Mary L .... part of	247	25
Wiley, Matilda A. and Frances A	92	33
Williams, Edgar L	31	34
Witson, Mrs. Birdie .... part of	12	25
Williams, Edward	88	34
Williams, Robert	61	34
Williams, William O	113	34
Wilking, Anna Mary	3	34
Wright, Willis W	364	32
Wilson, Alfred H .... part of	36	15
Whitcomb, Jerome G .... part of	142	33
Wise, Mrs. Mary	155	33
Wilcox, Charles D .... part of	145	33
Williams, Eliza E .... part of	279	35
Wilkison, William	19	35
Wierhake, Louisa	49	35
Willig, Charles and Henrietta .... part of	143	35
Wilson, Anna M .... part of	30	12
Wiesser, John	236	35
Williamson, Edmund	123	35
Wright, Winfield Taylor	54	35
Winter, Rosina	38	37
Whitsit, John A. and Jessie S .... part of	168	32
Winter, John H	25	37
Winklemann, Albert .... part of	189	35
Witte, Mary	378	32
Wilson, Highland	41	37
Williams, John H	184	35
Wilson, Rosanna T .... part of	149	25
Williams, Caleb S .... part of	346	32
Wilson, James H	5	35

OWNERS' NAMES.	Lot No.	Section
Williams, Susan................................	81	37
Wilson, Alexander C. and Sarah O............ part of	272	35
Wilson, Sallie H..............................	66	36
Wright, Beulah L....................... part of	268	35
Wishmier, Christian F................... part of	76	3
Williams, William B...........................	23	38
Wildrick, William D.................... part of	223	35
Whitehead, William C. and Florence B...........	324	35
Wright, Mrs. Laura A.........................	157	36
Wiegman, Sophie M...........................	116	38
Whitthoft, Elizabeth J........................	132	38
Williamson, Ellen.............................	177	36
Wright, George P....................... part of	60	36
Wilkisou, Rebecca............................	70	37
Wickard, Willard S...........................	82	36
Wishard, George W...........................	84	14
Williams, Daniel G...................... part of	2	4
Wright, Sally Ann and Anna M............ part of	108	36
Wright, Benjamin C. and Granville S...... part of	108	36
Wiellmann, Elizabeth M.......................	144	37
Wilson, Charles W...................... part of	211	37
Willis, Isom T................................	151	37
Windhorst, August C.................... part of	52	39
Willis, Cassius M. Clay................. part of	9	39
Wright, W. G................................	194	25
Widner, Charles N............................	198	37
Wilson, Teludeius.............................	104	39
Wright, Anna H..............................	23	14
White, Kittie and Isaac M............... part of	76	39
Wilgus, Elizabeth M.................... part of	130	39
Wills, Hamilton B...................... part of	197	39
White, James W..............................	13	37
Whitehead, Rosa L...........................	189	39
Williams, Joel................................	116	39
Whitford, Henry Y..................... part of	173	39
Wilson, Silvester F............................	345	39
Wiles, Ella D.......................... part of	286	39
Wilhelm, Louisa A............................	450	39

OWNERS' NAMES.	Lot No.	Section
Wilson, Wealtha A...	453	39
Whitson, Tobias...	360	39
Wilgus, William...	142	25
Wilson, Emma...	358	37
Willett, Mary A. and Hattie... part of	361	37
Wright, Asbury P... part of	267	31
Wilson, Charles A...	407	39
Winter, James M... part of	73	19
Wilt, Mary...	355	37
Willis, George...	162	37
Wittlin, Albert...	178	37
Wilson, Hannah...	274	39
Wilding, Joan... part of	159	25
White, Susan J...	457	39
Wilson, Mrs. Elizabeth...	237	39
White, Hughes W... part of	121	2
Williams, David A...	462	39
White, Rt. Rev. John Hazen, Bishop Indiana, and his successors in office...	252	39
Wiles, Thomas H...	284	37
Wilson, Richard M... part of	529	39
Williamson, Charles D...	434	37
Wood, James, Sr., Heirs of...	117	2
Wood, Augustus D...	40	5
Woollen, Milton...	76	5
Woods, J. M...	15	16
Woollen, William W...	22	12
Woodburn, James H... part of	201	16
Woollen, William W...	27	4
Wolfram, Christian...	13	19
Wolf, Catherine... part of	97	15
Wolf, William N...	84	19
Woelz, Louisa... part of	4	17
Wood, Phoebe E...	81	25
Woodruff, Henry D...	26 and 27	32
Woodard, Ferdinand, Heirs of...	83 and 84	32
Woodford, Tenie...	79 and 80	32
Woerner, Frederick...	212	18

CROWN HILL CEMETERY.

OWNERS' NAMES.	Lot No.	Section
Wocher, Regina	160	27
Woolen, Keziah	78	33
Wood, James W............part of	172	33
Wolfe, Annie E............part of	110	33
Wolfram, Sarah, Chas. A., Albert T. and Ernest E..part of	23	19
Woerner, Wilhelmina............sub 2	82	17
Wood, Edmonson R............part of	172	33
Worley, Albert F.	136	35
Wood, William E. and John B.	162	32
Woerner, Charles............part of	253	35
Woodward, James B.	79	37
Woodruff, Maggie A	183	38
Wood, John B.	37	36
Wonnell, Charles	370	38
Wooley, Josephine............part of	328	35
Worman, William	17	36
Wolf, Elizabeth............part of	152	38
Wolf, Augusta............part of	332	38
Woodbridge, William	91	38
Woerner, Charles F............part of	82	21
Wood, Mrs. Sarah............part of	4	3
Woods, George S	390	37
Wood, Jacob S............part of	38	36
Wolf, Louisa	176	37
Woods, Kate S	62	27
Wolcott, Eben H	266	38
Worrall, Elizabeth L.	153	37
Woodruff, Henrietta............part of	194	39
Wood, John M............part of	129	27
Wulzen, Charles	171	31
Wulff, Conrad............part of	209	25
Wuest, Louis............part of	49 and 54	18
Wulf, Henry	51	3
Wynn, Mrs. W. I.	5	5
Wysong, Susanna	13	20
Wyatt, William D............part of	70	20
Wylie, Andrew	98	32
Wydman, Lucy E	255	35

OWNERS' NAMES.	Lot No.	Section
Yandes, Daniel, Sr.	32 and 33	6
Yachman, Herman	21	16
Yeager, Louisa	52	17
Yewell, Elizabeth .... part of	299	31
Yeatton, Frederick and George H	179	34
Yeager, Casper	52	37
Velgerhouse, Mary Van .... part of	166	38
Youart, John M	29	1
Vohn, James C	104	14
Young, Thomas J	125	4
Young, David D. .... part of	80	17
Yoke, Mrs. Isabel J.	181 and 182	25
Youngerman, George and Scott	270	32
Young, John .... part of	29	15
Youngman, Charles .... part of	363	32
Youtsey, Sarah	104	35
Youngman, William M. .... part of	2	12
Young, Sarah	2	16
Yoke, Charles .... part of	170	38
Young, Archibald A .... part of	266	36
Young, William H	259	37
Yount, Horace J.	420	36
Yundt, Joseph H	22	25
Yule, William .... part of	6	20
Yung, Louis	100	36
Zable, Charles	185	16
Zaph, Dora and Philip	47	22
Zambell, Andrew .... part of	285	38
Zahl, Charles .... part of	301	38
Zehringer, Caroline	31	17
Zeph, Emma .... part of	38	14
Zschech, Elizabeth .... part of	6	38
Zimmerman, Christopher	67	2
Ziegler, Louisa	197	18
Ziegler, Charles A .... sub 1	71	20
Zismer, Paul M	186	35
Zimmerman, Annie	19	38
Zion, Alonzo A.	85	36

OWNERS' NAMES.		Lot No.	Section
Zwissler, Adam		96	38
Zimmerman, Fred		136	37
Zink, John	part of	181	39
Zimmer, Cecelia	part of	175	33
Zimmer, Ida A.	part of	175	33
Ziegel, Edward F.		169	39
Ziegler, August and Katie	...	214	39
Zobbe, Christian F.	part of	45	14
Zumpie, William	part of	234	25

www.ingramcontent.com/pod-product-compliance
Lightning Source LLC
Chambersburg PA
CBHW031813220426
43662CB00007B/628